fix your back

To my husband Ric and my children Alex and Ben

Published by ABC Books for the
AUSTRALIAN BROADCASTING CORPORATION
GPO Box 9994 Sydney NSW 2001

First published March 2002

National Library of Australia
Cataloguing-in-Publication entry
Bouvier, Anna-Louise.
  Fix your back.
  ISBN 0 7333 1069 9.
  1. Back - Care and hygiene. 2. Backache - Exercise therapy.
  I. Australian Broadcasting Corporation. II. Title.
617.56

Designed by vossdesign
Prepress by PageSet Victoria
Printed and bound in Australia by Shannon Books, Victoria

5 4 3 2 1

The exercises and advice given in this book are in no way intended as a substitute for
medical advice and guidance. Consult your doctor before beginning this or any other
exercise program. The author and publisher take no responsibility for any injury that
may be caused as a result of applying the information in this book.

fix your back

simple solutions
for painful problems

anna-louise bouvier

ABC
BOOKS

Contents

Part one
Balancing your spine

Part two
Supporting your core

Part three
Making you stronger

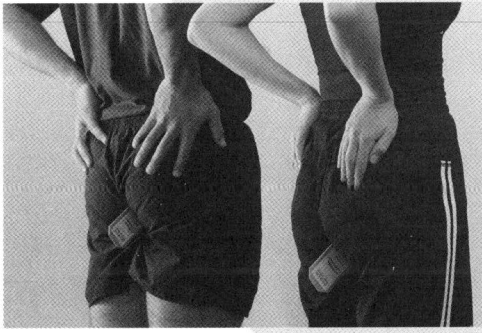

Preface

Back pain is frustrating.

I found it frustrating both personally and professionally. After 15 years in private practice treating patients with chronic back pain, I felt that there had to be a way to stop the typical cycle of years of grumbly, dull back pain, punctuated by acute episodes.

I injured my back at university when I was 19. Over the years I worked long hours with no time for treatment. I grew sick of having a dull ache in my back and intermittent bouts of sciatica. I felt out of control and at times depressed by the thought of how my back would end up. But through a combination of personal experience, observation of clients, teaching movement and education classes about back pain and reading the latest research, I learnt to fix my back. This book will show you how to fix yours.

One of the most annoying things about back pain is that those who have it often cannot discern a pattern between their good, pain-free days and their bad, achy days. Many of my clients wonder if perhaps they are imagining it, or if it is just a symptom of stress, as is suggested to them.

Unfortunately, living with pain leads to a debilitating lack of confidence. If people are unsure of what triggers off their pain or if they are at risk of further injury, they gradually limit their normal movement 'just in case'. Instead of helping, this actually creates more muscle imbalance as various other muscles are then recruited to compensate.

After spending a number of years listening to strikingly similar stories, I began to notice that there was a certain pattern to this kind of pain after all. It related not so much to how the pain began but rather to how it continued. What I noticed again and again was this tendency to restrict movement as the chronic, low-grade ache took hold.

Talking to patients about this led me to question them more about how they had moved in a past life, before they had back pain. I started to realise that certain types of people were more likely to develop long-term problems than others. This was mainly a result of how much flexibility they'd had when they were younger. Spines that had been very mobile were more at risk than stiffer spines.

Regardless of an individual's early flexibility, I found that the back pain of all my patients was aggravated by a sedentary life and too few opportunities to use the deep postural muscles that support the spine.

There has been a great deal of groundbreaking research into lower back pain and muscle imbalance in the last 10 years that has enhanced our understanding of what happens to muscles as a result of chronic pain. This includes research into hypermobility and injury and the role of the pelvic floor and the diaphragm in relation to the spine and stomach muscles.

Just as important are the findings on how our muscles learn new skills and acquire new habits. Research has shown that as people with lower back pain learn to compensate for weak muscles by recruiting others, so they have to activate the right muscles in order to move normally again. For people to retrain muscles they have to perform simple exercises repeatedly and receive feedback on their performance. This establishes the new muscular movements that eventually become habit.

The exercises must also be functional if they are to be adopted permanantly. For example, if you want to learn to turn on muscles that allow you to sit comfortably for longer, you have to practise that exercise while you sit, not while you are lying down. All the strategies in this book have been devised according to these principles.

The Physiocise method that I developed combines these various elements. It takes account of early spine mobility, muscle imbalance, movement restriction and postural weakness arising from a sedentary life. It also applies the latest research into chronic lower back pain and retraining muscle in the innovative program of exercises and strategies. It has proved highly successful with lots of people who thought they were going to have to put up with back pain for good.

The Physiocise framework outlined in this book provides you with a clear action plan for understanding why you have lower back pain and what strategies are right for you to fix it. The strategies are simple and functional but powerful and effective. They can be easily incorporated into your daily life to give you a whole new way of thinking about your body and a balanced, supported and strong spine.

You can break the cycle. You can fix your back. Here's how.

a common story

Your spine is like the internal foundation and framework of a building. Just like a building, it needs to be strong and secure. Your alignment is crucial to ensuring this stability and avoiding back pain. In this section we look at alignment and provide several fail-safe strategies to get you standing and sitting tall, strong and pain free.

Life in the 21st century

Life in the 21st century is a disaster for spines – we sit too much and move too little. While technology has brought fantastic benefits to our lives, it has also made us more sedentary. This is one of the main reasons back pain affects 8 out of 10 people in the Western world.

The way we work and live, and the way we move – or rather don't move – has changed a great deal. Our grandparents' generation was generally much stronger than we are. Women worked manually doing heavy washing and wringing out clothes. They walked more and did more physical labour through housework and caring for children. Many men also worked in much more labour intensive jobs.

Cars (if they owned one) didn't have power steering, but rather heavy steering wheels which needed a certain strength to control. Even to wind a window in the car took some physical strength. Typewriters were still heavy to use, with each press of a key needing considerable muscle work in the fingers and a good work out of the arm to push the carriage across at the end of each line.

Posture was important. Children were told to sit up straight, stand tall and keep their elbows off the table. Schools taught deportment and marching. Children walked, ran or rode to and from school and after school were encouraged to play outside, climb trees or just run around. In school playgrounds there were perilous looking monkey bars, tyres hanging from trees and climbing frames that were conquered daily. School desks largely had bench seats with angled desktops which encouraged straight spines. This environment was conducive to the strong postural muscles that would form the basis of their back strength for the rest of their lives.

The furniture of the 1940s and 1950s also encouraged good posture. 1950s furniture was very upright, couches were firm, chairs were hard – you couldn't slump even if you wanted to! And then the 1960s hit. The emerging attitude of 'let it all hang out' gradually changed our whole lifestyle. Forget standing straight in Doris Day dresses with pert breasts, carefully coiffed hair and belted frocks. Out went bras and belts, in came kaftans and long hair, along with the slump that reflected the laid back attitude of this generation.

Back pain affects 8 out of 10 people.

Our push-button world lets us do more while moving less.

So too, furniture began to reflect this attitude with bean bags, bucket seats and modular lounges. As we sank deep into our new comfort zone, the beginning of the posture disaster took hold.

By the 1970s the new commercial realities of mass seating saw the advent of stackable, moulded plastic seating. Schools embraced plastic bucket seats and flat high desks as a cheap, functional and light alternative to the old style heavy wooden desks. But in that one decision, children's posture was doomed as the only way to sit in one of those seats was to slump. Unconsciously, most children relieved the discomfort caused by sitting in that position by swinging on the front two legs of their chair (which allowed them to sit with a beautifully straight spine). But as this caused the chairs to break, most teachers stopped this quick smart! So, instead of six hours a day in a relatively good sitting position, which subtly built up the muscle corset of back and stomach muscles vital for good posture, children were now spending many hours in a rounded, slumped position. This was probably the beginning of the loss of the deep muscle base of this generation.

As technology of every description became more sophisticated, a great number of jobs became more sedentary. Through the late 1980s and early 1990s repetitive strain injury (RSI) was prevalent. The new lighter keyboards meant that we began using a few tiny muscles in our hands over and over again. Sitting posture also contributed to this problem, so we designed ergonomic chairs to help us sit perfectly straight. But if we couldn't touchtype, we still needed to look up and down at the keyboard and the screen all day and no chair was going to prevent our spines from curving.

Technology continues to find ways to make our daily tasks easier. Cordless touch phones, the garage door opener, power steering and electric windows, the TV remote control, these and many more devices are robbing us of chances to make the bigger arm and trunk muscles work harder during the course of a normal day. And because everything has to happen faster, we don't have time to walk, so we drive more. By the beginning of the 21st Century we are spending more time on our bottoms than on our feet.

We spend more time on our bottoms than on our feet.

Why is back pain so

It seems now we have a back pain epidemic. Everyone you talk to has it or knows someone who has it. It appears to be affecting people of all ages from teenagers to people in their 50s and 60s. Why has it become so prevalent?

The main reason is the enormous change in our lifestyle and work environments brought about by technological advances. Far from having increased leisure time, we have increased the amount of time we spend sitting and working. When we are not at work, we continue to be sedentary. Exercise is relegated to a small portion of the day and requires substantial motivation to maintain. These conditions lead gradually to **muscle imbalance**: fewer muscles doing more work, tight muscles that are never stretched and weak muscles that are never challenged. This creates huge potential for injury. Once this occurs, small injuries can develop into chronic problems that take months, if not years, to settle. Even in the absence of an obvious injury, people get used to living with low-grade pain much of the time and cannot see how to effectively change the situation.

prevalent?

Another important reason is because we are becoming weaker at a younger age. Instead of riding bikes or walking home, children are picked up in the car or go home on buses because of distance or danger. Working parents are obliged to place their children in after school programs that provide more structured time, with less opportunity for unstructured play like climbing trees or just running around. The increasing pressures of school work at younger and younger ages often means that children need to do hours of homework, which necessitates even more sitting. Any parent knows that it can be a struggle encouraging children to play outside rather than spend hours 'relaxing' in front of TV, Gameboys, computers and Nintendos. It all adds up to more sitting, more slumping – fewer muscles working in younger and younger kids.

Good posture in children wasn't just achieved through activity, it was also brought about by all those reminders that most of us remember hating! Now that parents are working harder and longer outside the home and have so much to 'nag' children about at the end of the day, 'sit up straight, shoulders back, elbows off the table' messages have become one of the casualties of our faster and more pressured lives.

The good news is we can make changes that allow us to take control of our back pain. It is possible to fix your back! The first step is to think about what your day involves. Often just becoming conscious of something is enough to bring about a subtle change in behaviour that can lead to a big improvement.

It is possible to fix your back.

The activity diary

Do you know which activities you engage in regularly that could be affecting your back? Using muscles in a particular way (or rather not using them) leads to weakness, tightness and eventually pain. This is where many of our problems start.

Understanding how the demands of your life affect your back is an essential first step to fixing your pain. An activity diary can help you with this. Start in the morning of your average day and go through your day – really try to think about what you do, or perhaps don't do, in your week.

The following activity diary shows five days in the life of an average, sedentary, working person. I find that women with young children at home tend to do significantly more physical activity.

Women also do more of the cooking and cleaning in the house. Men on the other hand tend to have more 'spurt' activity on their charts, such as outdoor projects and weekend physical work, but less consistent physical activity during their week.

You can see this person sits almost three times as much as they stand and move in any one day.

Many people think that they must have done something to have started their back pain and feel frustrated when they can't

The sedentary part of the day

Activity	Do I sit to do this?	Number of hours per day
Going to work	Yes	0.5
At work	A lot	8
Going home from work	Yes	0.5
At home at night	Yes, TV or reading paper or using computer	3
Total per average day		**12 hours**

The non-sedentary part of the day

Activity	What do I do	Number of hours per day
Before work	Getting dressed, tidying house, helping with children	1
At work	Walking to get lunch, going to bathroom/photocopier	1
Formal exercise	Walking 30 minutes two mornings (60 minutes in 5 days)	12 minutes average
After work	Washing, helping with meals	2 hours
Total per average day		**4.20 hours**

remember a specific incident. In fact, sitting too much is often the problem. Even though it seems as if you're not doing much when you sit, the muscles of your spine and stomach are working hard to hold you up against gravity. If the muscles aren't strong enough to support you, sitting places a great load on your spine and over time this leads to pain.

For some people the problem may not be sitting. Their activity diary may show they are doing too much of the same movement over and over. Mothers with young children are a classic example. They are bending down to lift, bending into cots, bending forward washing and cleaning up, bending into bath tubs. Looking at their activity diary, they can see that there is very little movement to balance all the bending, which leads to problems and pain.

Creating a framework

How come not everyone has the same back pain?

Analysing your own body – working out how you move, how you were designed to move and what your muscles like to do – is the next important step in fixing your back. Many elements make up each individual's problem. It's a bit like a jigsaw puzzle – at the moment all the pieces seem to make no sense. But as we slowly put the puzzle together it will not only become clearer, you will see it is also quite simple.

So they have acupuncture on Mondays, chiropractic on Tuesdays, a massage on Thursdays and do yoga or Pilates three times a week – yet they are still getting pain.

You can make back pain complex and technical, or you can make it simple and logical. Fixing back pain is like great cooking, where a few simple ingredients used in the right order and with enough time and thought creates the perfect dish. But just because something is simple doesn't mean it is simplistic.

Back pain solutions have tended to go in 'flavour of the month' cycles. The latest craze is 'core stability' so suddenly everyone is desperately working on their tummy muscles. A few years ago it was the Alexander Technique, working on balance and posture. The gym craze focused on getting stronger and fitter. Years ago we had laminectomies, then paw paw injections to shrink discs, then manipulation – the list is endless. From faith healers to weight training there is always someone with the 'cure' for back pain. There is value in nearly all these things, and in some more than others. They are all probably part of the solution to the puzzle. But to get help with your particular story you need to think logically about what will help when.

You can make back pain complex and technical, or you can make it simple and logical.

Some people try a succession of different therapies to fix their back pain, and frustratingly none offer long-term relief. They try a new approach, which initially helps a little. Then they have another episode, they seem to be back to where they started and they conclude that another method didn't work. In fact, what they tried might be a useful therapy for certain types of pain, but was not right for them at that stage.

Alternatively, they try what I call the napalm approach, the let's-throw-everything-at-this-and-get-rid-of-it-for-good approach (surprisingly, more men tend to use this approach!). So they have acupuncture on Mondays, chiropractic on Tuesdays, a massage on Thursdays and do yoga or Pilates three times a week – yet they are still getting pain.

The difference with the Physiocise approach is the framework. Many of the strategies are things you may have been told before. How you put them together, when to use them and why is what makes the difference. It is not unlike reconstructing a building that has suffered structural damage after an earthquake. You first realign it and make sure all the bits are sitting on top of one another.

Then you look at the core and the foundation and make sure they are stable and supported. Finally, and only then, do you work on the outer cladding to make sure that the whole thing can withstand external forces. Unless you work on each step and get that right, chances are the whole thing will keep collapsing.

The framework I recommend for fixing your back involves three steps, each one critical to the next:

I Balance
Balancing your spine

2 Support
Supporting your core

3 Strength
Making you stronger

Balancing your spine

The first step of the Physiocise framework is balancing your spine.
By learning to align your spine correctly, your muscles have the chance
to work more efficiently.

Many people first try to strengthen their backs without balancing the forces of the spine, causing the muscles to work harder than they should. If the spine is well balanced it takes fewer forces to hold it up against gravity. That's all good posture is – your spine holding itself up against gravity.

When our earliest ancestors came out of the caves, their spines had not yet developed the back and buttock muscles to hold them up against gravity, so they slumped around looking more like apes than humans. As we evolved and spent more time upright and walking around, we developed stronger back and buttock muscles to hold us up and our posture became more upright. Not only were we balanced against gravity but we also had the postural muscles to hold us there. But as we now spend more time sitting than moving, we have gradually lost some of those muscles that are good for holding us up. You only have to take a good look at your bottom to know that you probably don't use it much!

To redevelop those postural muscles we need to teach our spines to balance again. If you get your head balanced between your shoulders, your chest balanced over your hips, your weight even between your feet, then your muscles aren't going to have to work nearly so hard to hold you there. But if you try to strengthen your back muscles when you are still sitting and standing like a gorilla, you will find keeping your muscles switched on for any length of time impossible. That's one of the reasons people find maintaining good posture so impossible.

Sitting and standing for any length of time need not be exhausting. It's all about balance. You need to learn how your spine tends to align itself. At its most basic level standing posture can be divided into two main categories: the **sway back** and the **slumper**. Look in the mirror and see which one looks more like you. One posture is not better than the other, it's just that each posture tends to make certain muscles tighter and others weaker. You may also have a subtle sideways curve (**scoliosis**) which further complicates your alignment. So you could be a sway back with a sideways curve, or a slumper with a sideways curve.

The well-balanced spine takes fewer forces to hold it upright.

How does your spine align?

The sway back

More common in women and girls, the classic sway back looks a little like this. Often having done ballet, gymnastics or dancing as children, a sway back's classic standing position is bottom out and feet turned out (a bit like 1st position in ballet). If you are a sway back you'll also often struggle with your tummy popping out!

From the waist up, your posture is usually quite good, but from the waist down you have problems. When sitting you also tend to over-sway in the low back, so sitting for any length of time usually makes you very achy. Sometimes to relieve the pressure you slump the other way, just to take the load off.

Are you a sway back?

- my tummy tends to pop out
- my feet tend to turn out
- I have tight muscles at the front of my hip
- I have tight calf muscles
- I am generally flexible with the exception of my hips and calves

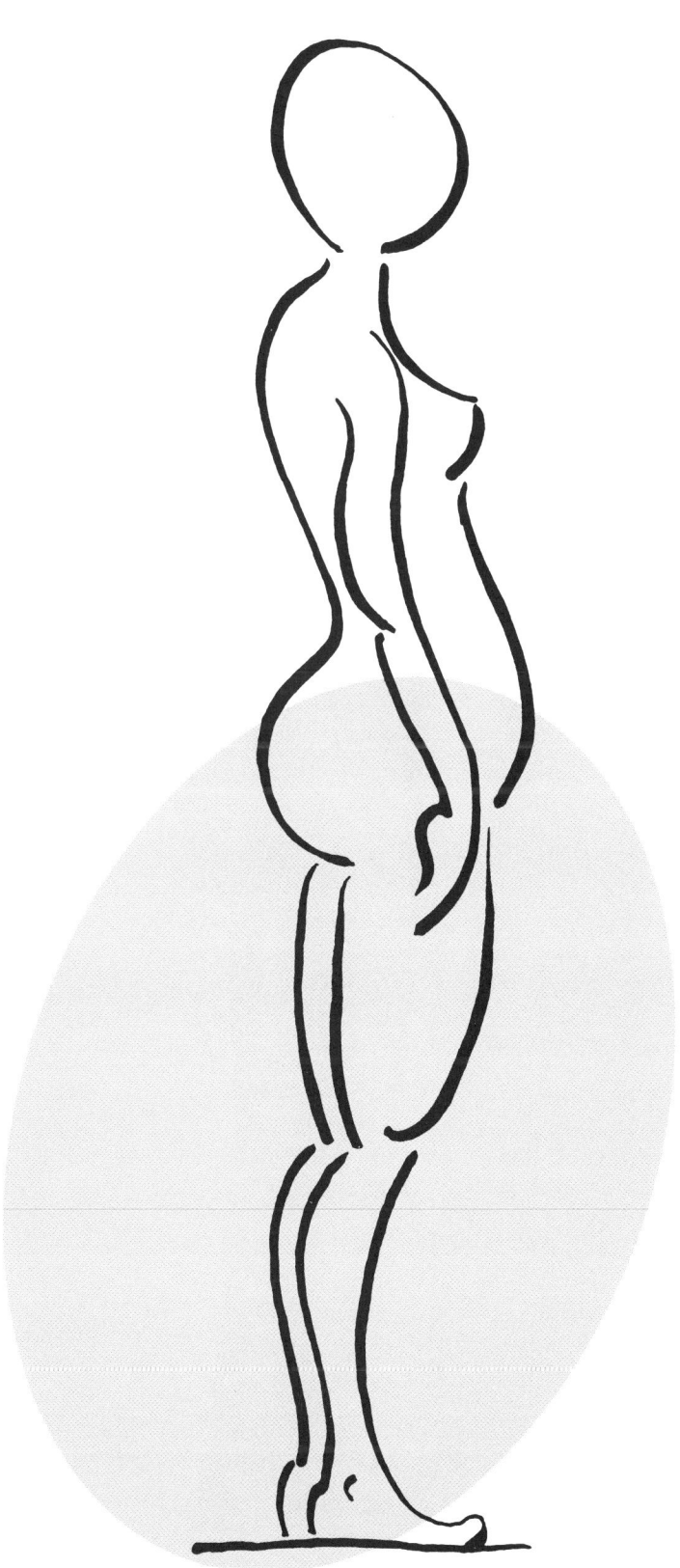

If you have a very
sway back, all the
balance exercises
are very important
for you.

Establishing awareness of your posture,
and constantly reminding yourself to find
your balance point is most important. If
you have a very sway back, all the balance
exercises are very important for you.
Initially, you'll need to focus on reminding
yourself about balancing yourself – you'll
find that just when you've got those feet
straight and your bottom tucked under,
you'll forget and find they've sneaked
out again. Some of this is because the
muscles in your hips may be tight as
they have held your back and legs in this
position for years. These may need some
specific stretching, which is covered in
Part 2.

The slumper

Slumping is the way most of us stand after prolonged periods.

The arms crossed over the tummy, the shoulders rounding, the bottom disappearing and the neck poked forward. It makes us look a hundred years old but it just feels too difficult to stand any other way. You know that horrible feeling when you catch sight of yourself in a shop window and you realise that your head is sitting about 10 cm in front of your chest. That's the slumper in action.

Are you a slumper?

- I am stiff between the shoulder blades
- I am tight in my hamstrings
- my tummy tends to spread
- my breathing tends to be shallow
- I have a flat bottom

Years of slumping produces all sorts of changes to your muscles.

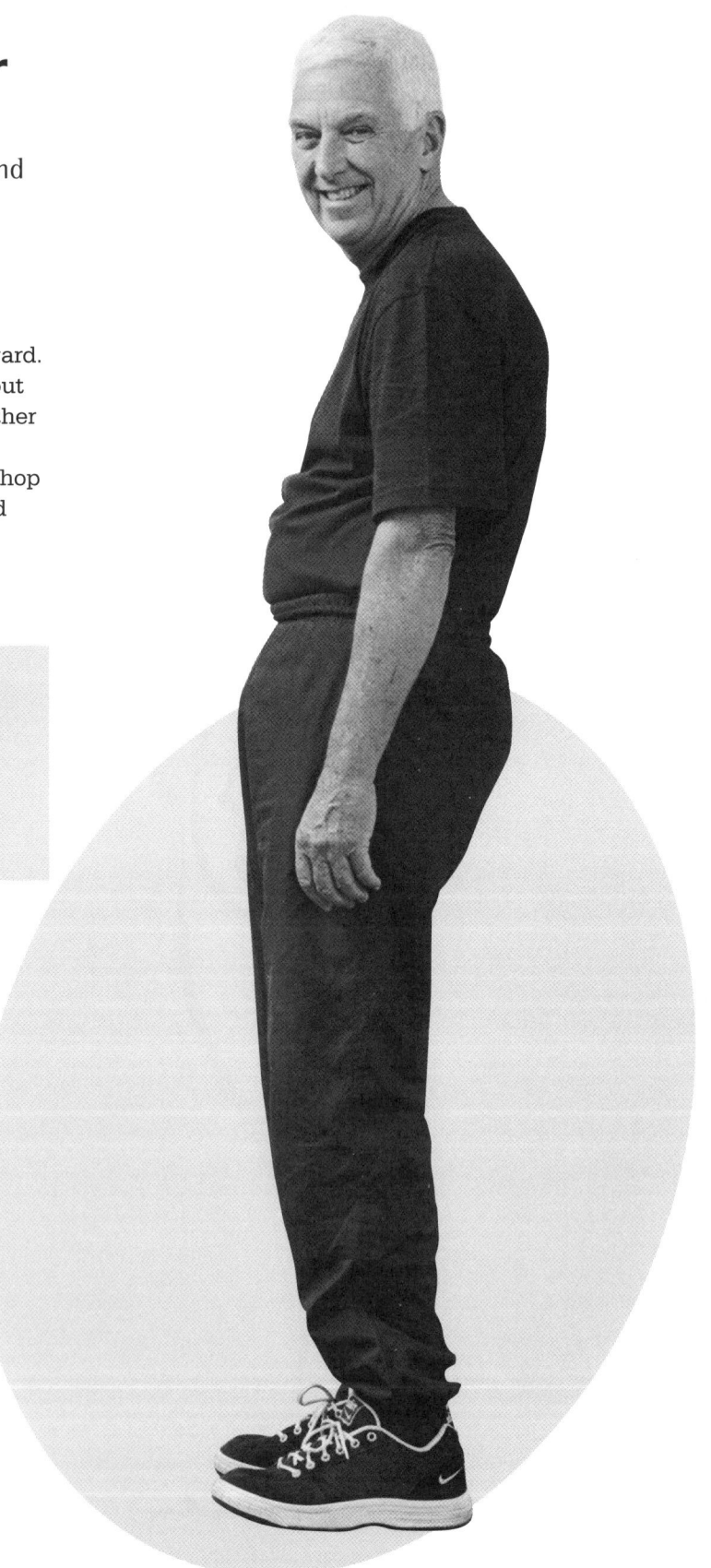

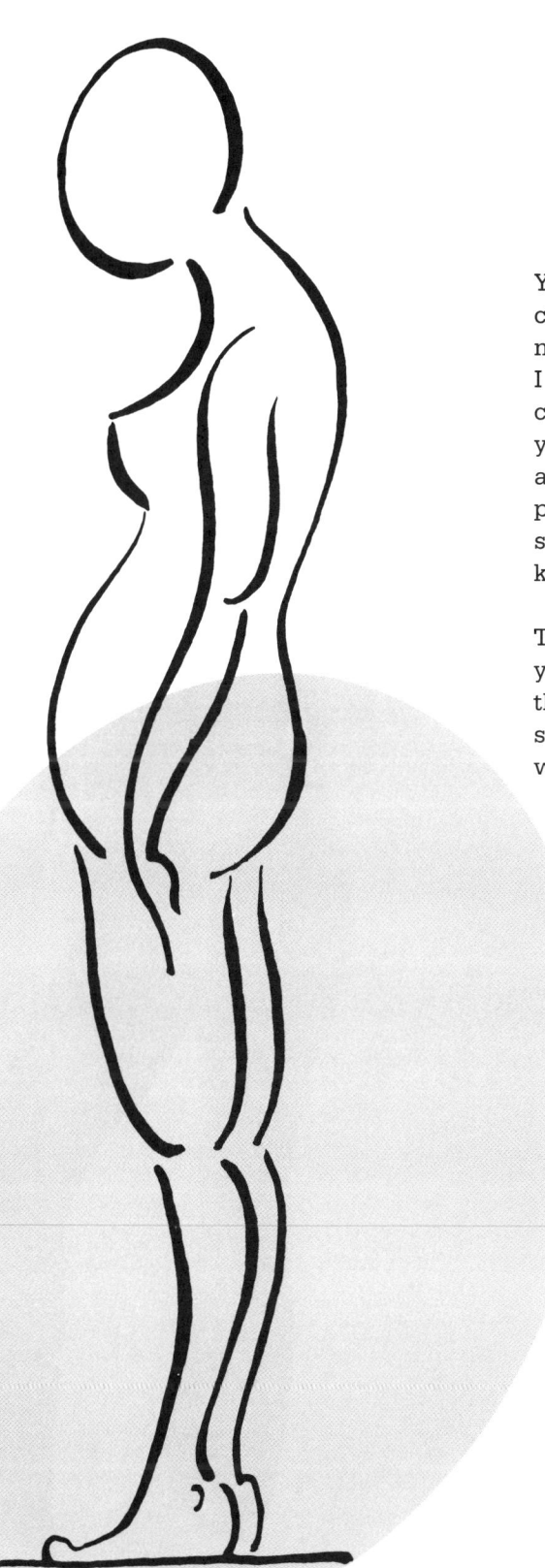

Years of slumping produces all sorts of changes to your muscles. Gradually you notice your buttocks dropping (a condition I call blancmange buttocks), your chest collapsing, your tummy spreading and your shoulders drooping. Every once in a while you try to haul your chest up and put your shoulders back but within a few seconds it feels exhausting and before you know it you're back down again.

The good news is, once you realise that you slump and you find out how to use the balance strategies, sitting and standing tall is not nearly the hard work you think it is.

The sideways curver

The sideways curver finds that one shoulder seems higher than the other. This is actually the result of a slight curve in the spine tipping the chest slightly sideways and changing the level of the shoulders, known as **scoliosis.**

Mild scoliosis is widespread. Some people were born with it, called **structural scoliosis**. Structural scoliosis typically affects the bones in the midback of the spine between the shoulder blades. All it means is that instead of all the bones in your spine sitting perfectly straight, one on top of the other, some sit very slightly off to the side. Over a few levels this creates a slight sideways curve. Bit by bit the structural position of the spine creates the muscle imbalance.

Postural scoliosi*s* is also common and develops as a result of doing something too often on one side. Lugging heavy schoolbags on one shoulder, carrying children on one hip, or jobs such as dentistry which necessitate bending and twisting to one side, can all contribute to creating a postural scoliosis where the muscle imbalance gradually creates the curve in the spine.

Both sway backs and slumpers can have scoliosis.

Most people don't realise they have scoliosis. This is no big drama, but it does tend to make the muscles on one side slightly tighter than the other. It also changes your ability to balance your spine, because one side will tend to drop down and forward. Many women struggle with having uneven shoulders without knowing why. They will find that one bra strap always drops off one shoulder (this is usually the side they lean to, with the lower shoulder) and they tend to carry their shoulder bags on the other 'higher' shoulder, because it doesn't slip off.

Standing with your weight more on one leg than the other may be another reason for this sideways unevenness. Again this can be structural (you actually have a physically longer bone in your leg relative to the other side) or it may be postural (over the years you have always tended to stand on one side and gradually the muscles on one side are much tighter and appear to make the leg shorter).

Whatever the reason for the scoliosis, the secret is to find out how you stand and balance. If it is postural imbalance (and most of these imbalances are) then gradually, by constantly putting yourself in a better position, you can change your muscle imbalance and take the uneven forces off your spine. Ultimately this means less pain and less work for your poor old muscles trying to hold you up!

The following two simple tests will help you find out whether you have scoliosis and how you stand and balance. You need to look at yourself front on in the mirror when you do them.

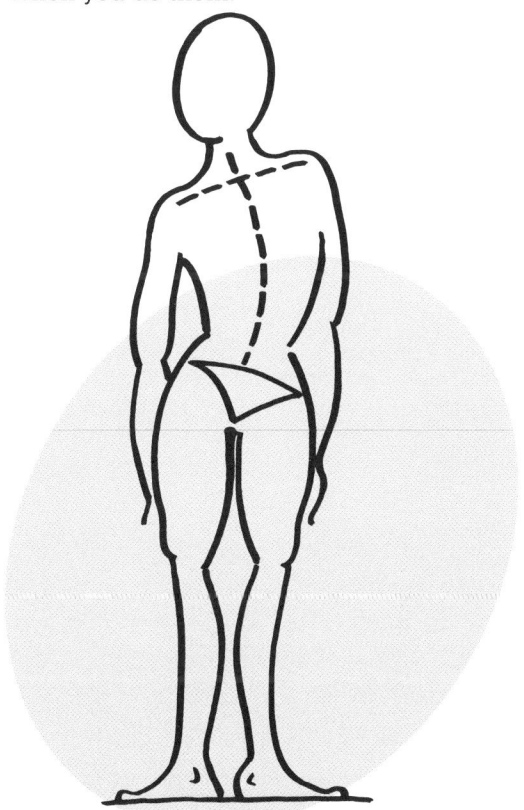

One shoulder higher than the other test

Starting position

● Stand in front of a mirror, preferably without a top on, with both feet parallel and about 30cm apart.

The movement

● Lift your chest slightly and then look at the level of the points of your shoulders.
You may see immediately that one shoulder is slightly dropped compared to the other

● Look at the distance between the base of your neck and the point of the shoulder on the same side. Now compare this with the distance between the base of the neck and the point of the shoulder on the other side. You may see that one distance is much less. This is your higher shoulder. Now look at your waist on the side of the lower shoulder. You will probably notice that you are more dropped on this side and that the angle of your waist is more acute on that side. This is all due to that slight sideways bend in your spine.

What you can do about it

● Be aware that you tend to drop to that side.

● Look carefully at all the balancing strategies especially the ones related to lifting and carrying.

Standing evenly test

Starting position

● Stand with your feet parallel and your weight evenly distributed over your feet.
Notice how this feels.

The movement

● Shift your weight onto your left leg more than your right.
Does that feel familiar and comfortable?

● Now shift your weight onto your right leg more than your left.
Does that feel more familiar and comfortable than the previous weight distribution?

What you can do about it

● If you stand more on your right leg than your left, your spine will tend to drop to the
left and your left shoulder will also drop. This makes trying to keep the forces on your
spine when you stand or sit very difficult. If you stand with more weight on your left,
the opposite usually happens – your right shoulder drops.

● It's a matter of becoming more and more aware of keeping yourself lined up and balanced.
To start with it will feel weird and at times uncomfortable, because your muscles are not used
to that position. In time they will become more used to balancing and that will give your deep
postural muscles a chance to learn to switch on.

For some people, just learning about balancing their spine is enough to change their posture and relieve their pain. The balancing strategies in Part 1 will help you find simple ways to make it easier to sit, stand, walk and carry – all by understanding about balance and alignment. Even if you have never had pain, learning about balancing is one of the best ways to maintain your posture and prevent injury.

For many people, however, this is only the first step – you can barely find your balance point before you lose it again. This is because some people's spines are floppier than others, and the floppier you are the harder it is to hold yourself against gravity.

Supporting your core is the next step in helping maintain this new alignment. How hard this is depends on whether you are a floppy, a stiffy or a flippy.

Supporting your core

The second step of the Physiocise framework is supporting your core. Different spines need different levels of support. Some people's spines are floppy while other people's are very stiff. Establishing whether you're a **floppy**, **stiffy** or **flippy** will help you find out why you experience pain and what you can do about it.

The bones of our skeleton are held together by semi-elastic cords called ligaments. These deep structures bind bone to bone to form joints. We are held stable and upright against gravity by a series of deep muscles that wrap around our skeleton, particularly in our lower back and neck. These muscles form natural corsets.

Ligaments are like the cords that connect all the pieces of a Pinocchio string puppet. Their flexibility differs from individual to individual, but broadly speaking we can be divided into three physical types: floppies, stiffies and flippies. The type of ligaments you are born with determines your type.

Floppies are born with loose ligaments. That's why if you're a floppy you can stretch and do backbends. But you also rely heavily on your deep muscle corsets to hold you up and keep you stable. You need to support your core by stabilising your wobbly bits.

Stiffies are the opposite of floppies, as they are born with very tight ligaments. If you are a stiffy, it is likely that you hate stretching. The major advantage of your physical type is that you do not rely so much on your deep muscle corsets to hold you up as a floppy. You need to support your core by stretching your stiff bits.

Flippies are somewhere in-between: flippies are floppies with stiff bits! Generally they are born with ligaments that are more flexible in some joints than others, which can lead to alignment problems. If you're a flippy you need to ensure your deep muscle corsets support your wobbly bits, but you also need to stretch your stiff bits.

There are many gradations between the three categories. We all fit somewhere along a sliding scale, with the great majority of us being flippies. Those on the left of the scale are floppier and are most likely to develop back pain, as supporting their core is very difficult. Decide where you think you sit on the scale to work out your main priorities for supporting your core.

Floppies	Flippies		Stiffies
	Floppier flippies	Stiffer flippies	
Need to stabilise your wobbly bits.	Need to work on stabilising your wobbly bits more than stretching your stiff bits.	Need to work on stretching your stiff bits more than stabilising your wobbly bits.	Need to stretch your stiff bits.

Floppies need a great deal of support and stability.

Are you a floppy?

As a child:

- I found stretching easy.
- I could do (or almost do) the splits.
- I could do back bends.
- People said I was double-jointed
- My joints clicked a lot.

If you have two or more 'yes' answers, you are probably a floppy.

Extreme floppies only make up about 8 per cent of the population. They are more commonly women, who as children were attracted to ballet and gymnastics, but some men can also have floppy tendencies, especially those who hurdled or did high jump. These people started life as fit floppies – flexible, dynamically strong and stable.

Floppies are also susceptible to what I call 'message-too-late injuries'. One function of ligaments is to prevent joints from moving too far and dislocating the skeleton. The ligaments carry tiny warning receptors, which send a message to the brain to activate the muscles to protect the joint. Because floppies have ligaments that are more like bungy cords than tight elastic bands, that stretch point is often exceeded and the brain receives the message too late.

If you're a floppy in trouble your deep muscles are no longer working well, either due to injury, poor posture, too much sitting or a combination of all three. You don't feel flexible at all, in fact your muscles feel tight all the time and achy. When sitting at the movies or in a plane, you constantly change position to get comfortable. You're up, then down, then crossing and uncrossing your legs every few minutes – your brain keeps sending messages that these muscles are tired and to use something else. This is all part of the muscle system trying to compensate and provide some of the stability you have lost.

Are you a floppy in trouble?

- My acute bouts of pain have increased but I also seem to have some dull achy pain much of the time.
- I often feel stiff and tight, and constantly need to stretch or click to relieve pain and tension.
- Compared with most people I look flexible, but compared with what I used to be able to do, I'm tight.
- Sitting, standing or doing anything for for any length of time is difficult.
- When the pain is bad I need to keep changing position.
- Mornings aren't great – I get out of bed feeling tight but generally feel better after a hot shower.
- There just doesn't seem to be a pattern. One day I'm great, the next day terrible for no real reason.
- I often have neck problems, with reasonably frequent headaches.

If you have answered 'yes' more than three times, it's time to stabilise.

stiffies

Are you a stiffy?

As a child:

- I hated stretching.
- I was never able to bend past my knees.
- Touching my toes with my knees straight was impossible.
- I always had a very short stride when I ran.

If you have two or more 'yes' answers, you are probably a stiffy.

You'll know straight away if you're a stiffy. You hate stretching and have always hated anything to do with flexibility. It's not that you weren't sporty as a child, often you were – you just didn't enter the high jump.

If you're a stiffy you often get away with being slack in your deep muscles without getting much pain because muscles aren't as important for supporting your spine. Your posture may look generally awful, often quite slumpy, but it doesn't change much from sitting to standing. Because of those tight connecting ligaments even when you try to slump you don't go far.

Instead of fluctuations in pain, your pain is more consistent. Your body tells you you've gone too far when you reach the end of your flexibility. No message-too-late-injuries for you – if anything, the message comes too soon! Surprisingly, you often bend quite well as you have to bend your knees to pick anything up off the floor, otherwise you'd never reach it and this does give you some protection.

Trying to find a balance point is like trying to haul up the leaning tower of Pisa – seemingly impossible if you're a stiffy. Your body needs some movement, the aching you feel is sending you a message. You need to stretch even though you would rather not! To support your core you need to stretch the things that keep pulling you out of position. Once you know what to do it's not hard to stretch – with a few simple stretches, your back will respond quickly.

Are you a stiffy in trouble?

- My back feels stiff all the time.
- I get out of bed with very little movement.
- I remember an incident that started my backpain.
- I am also noticing a few shoulder, knee or elbow problems.
- My posture is getting worse but I find it impossible to straighten up.

If you have answerd 'yes' more than three times, it's time to get stretching.

Stiffies need to stretch.

Are you a flippy?

As a child:

- I could touch my toes fairly easily but could never do the splits.
- I was reasonably flexible but always had tight hamstrings (the muscles at the back of the legs).
- I always felt a bit stiff between my shoulder blades.

If you have two or more 'yes' answers, you are probably a flippy.

Most people fall into the category of flippies, although some are floppier flippies than others. As children they may have been flexible but couldn't usually do the splits. Like floppies, flippies rely heavily on their muscles to support their core. They experience similar patterns to floppies in trouble, but without the huge fluctuations and often without the intense pain. The main difference is that if you're a flippy you'll have stiff bits that floppies don't have and those bits can differ from one side to the other.

The stiff bits are generally the result of scoliosis (whether postural or structural).This means that some bits become stiffer and place more load on the deep muscle corsets. The combination of wobbly bits and stiff bits means that the wobbly bits need muscular support (like floppies) and the stiff bits need stretching (like stiffies).

Flippies need a combination program of stabilising and stretching.

The stiff bits are usually in the base of the neck through to the mid-back and the muscles at the back of the leg (the hamstrings and calves). The wobbly bits are usually the deep muscles that should be holding us up, in particular the low back corset.

The stiff bits need to be stretched. Furthermore, you need to focus on stretching the side that feels tighter to realign the load on the spine. Although this stretching will feel good, it is not enough. To fix your back for good, you need to develop better support in your deep muscle corsets.

Are you a flippy in trouble?

- I tend to stand on one leg.
- One shoulder tends to drop forward.
- My tummy tends to pop out.
- I'm reasonably flexible, but I feel tight between my shoulder blades and at the back of my legs.
- Stretching and moving my back eases my pain, but it doesn't last.
- I feel quite tight in the mornings.
- Sitting or standing for any length of time is difficult.
- I'm starting to notice neck pain.

If you have answerd 'yes' more than three times, you need to stabilise and stretch.

flippies

Using your stabilisers

The first major component of supporting your core is stabilising any wobbly bits. This applies mainly to floppies or flippies who are more flexible, but all body types also need to ensure they are stable.

Stabilising something is very different from just making it stronger. To make something really stable it needs to be able to stay in place for long periods of time, not just for short bursts.

We have two types of muscles – **postural** and **phasic**. Our postural (stabilising) muscles are designed to switch on for a long time, at a low grade, without getting tired. They are composed of 'tortoise' muscle fibres. They are particularly important when you have to do something for a long while without moving, such as sitting at a desk for hours, or standing in a queue. Even though you don't seem to be doing anything, there are lots of muscles working to keep your body stable: hence the term **stabilising** muscles.

Phasic muscles work in bursts when we need to do something more active. It's not that our postural muscles turn off, but that the phasic muscles come in as well. These are the sprint muscles and they are composed of 'hare' muscle fibres. They come in strongly but also get tired more quickly and need to rest.

When you have a combination of good postural muscles and strong phasic muscles you have what's called **dynamic stability**. This is the ultimate pain free goal. To help take the load off your spine, the phasic muscles you need to work on are the legs, buttocks, arms and shoulders. If doing things in one position is very difficult, your tortoise muscle may not be working as well as it should be. You may be able to do just about anything active (except perhaps heavy lifting), but the thought of having to sit for an hour, or go on a long car trip, would drive you crazy. If this is the case, retraining those stabilising muscles is essential. The spine needs them to support the load on its joints, ligaments and discs. If it doesn't have that support, down it flops and on comes the pain.

Floppies and floppier flippies rely heavily on the stabilising muscles for support because they were born with those loose connecting structures. Unfortunately these muscles are susceptible to injury and once any element of the stabilising system is affected, the whole tortoise pulls up for a rest. This is when the pain really starts.

More efficient tortoise muscle means better stability.

When you have a combination of good
postural muscles and strong phasic muscles
you have what's called 'dynamic stability' –
this is the ultimate pain free goal.

Your spine is held stable by two muscular
corsets. The first supports the low back
and spine, the second the neck and head.
Visualise old-fashioned corsets with layers
of supporting strings going in many
different directions. That's pretty much
how your body's corsets work – they are
made up of layers of muscle, each one
doing a different job. The deepest layers
have the most tortoise muscle and are
critical for providing postural stability.

Retraining the lower back corset is an
important part of fixing your back. This is
especially so because, not only does it have
the stomach muscles at the front, which
wrap around to join the deep back muscles
behind, but it also has a lid (the diaphragm)
and a floor (pelvic floor muscles). The
diaphragm and pelvic floor muscles are
in themselves critical features of this deep
muscle corset. Learning to breathe well
will help you maintain stability in your core.

You'll find that as you start practising your
strategies, all these elements will start to
make your back feel better and you'll feel
more comfortable.

While floppier spines are more likely to
develop back pain, there is some good
news. As floppies get older they can also
get a bit stiffer. This means that they rely
less on their deep muscle corsets for
stability and the pain tends to ease off.
The peak age for back pain is typically
from the mid-20s to the early 50s. After
this, stretching is important to relieve
stiffness, but back pain is usually no
longer such a problem.

The importance of stretching

The second major component of supporting your core is stretching any stiff bits. The stiffer your spine the more you need to stretch.

Muscles can be tight because they're 'structurally' tight. For example, if a woman wears high heels all day every day her calf muscles will become shorter because the brain perceives that's all the length they need.

Stretching structurally tight muscles, either because you've used them in a certain position over and over, or because you were born a stiffy or because you have some stiff bits, is hard and slow work. The good news is, if you do it often enough and in the right way, it can be very effective.

Muscles can also become tight as a result of muscle spasm. This feels completely different and is a bit like clenching your fist for an hour. It's a slow dull ache, forcing you to do something to try and ease it. That's when your body instinctively tries to stretch to ease that feeling of tightness. In floppies and floppier flippies who have lost their stabilisers due to injury, the body is adept at giving the spine the extra support and taking the load off by 'spasming' the back muscles. It's a primitive, and not very effective way your nerves and muscles try to give you some stability.

But because those muscles aren't designed to work that way, they get fatigued leaving you with a constant, nagging ache. Your natural instinct is to move and stretch to avoid the pain. Sometimes 'clicking' the joint underneath also relieves it for a few minutes.

While stretching and 'clicking' provides short term relief it won't last – the body has sent in that spasm for a reason. Unless there is some other support around the core to take the load off, after a while the muscles will go back into spasm and the pain will return.

As a short term solution, specific relieving stretches can be effective in easing the tension created by muscle spasm. For long term relief it's important to understand what that spasm means and why it's there. To stop the chronic cycle you need to stabilise the core and take the load off those joints, ligaments and discs.

If you are a stiffy, stretching is a critical part of fixing your back. This is not an easy path for you, but the results are worth the effort. For the first time in years you will have freedom of movement and less pain.

The good news is,
if you do it often
enough, stretching
can be very effective.

How much stretching?
This table tells you how often
you should stretch.

Floppies	Flippies		Stiffies
	Floppier flippies	Stiffer flippies	
For short term relief, use the stretches in Part 2 occasionally.	For short and medium term relief use the stretches in Part 2 at least three times a week.	For long term relief use the stretches in Part 2 daily.	Any movement is a bonus. Although hard work, you'll feel like a new person!

Making you stronger

The final component of the Physiocise framework is making you stronger. This will give you the confidence to move normally again. As you use your muscles more your muscle tone will also change.

Most of us, understandably, want to see results for all our hard work! By working on the first and second parts of the Physiocise framework, you will re-balance your body and build its internal foundation, while at the same time relieving any tension that might be pulling it back out of position. Then it is time to get to work on the cladding – the visible outer muscles.

Now you need to develop dynamic stability – the ability not only to sit or stand for longer periods but to lift, carry and bend without consciously protecting your back. For this you need to strengthen your limbs so they can take some of the load off your spine. Your legs in particular are like hydraulic systems, which bend and straighten to place your trunk where you want it. Not only do you have to think about doing this (because you know how you 'should' lift) but you have to use them in the right way over and over again until they develop that strength.

More support,
less fatigue,
less pain.

The other secret to developing your hydraulics is your bottom. Instead of resembling blancmange at the top of your thighs, your buttocks can be a powerhouse of support when used in the right way. Your arms and shoulders can also take a load off your neck and back.

The strategies in Part 3 for making you stronger are about the skill of using your muscles properly so that you'll use fewer more efficiently. And with that comes power and strength.

Fix your Back focuses on chronic, achy pain, not acute or inflammatory back pain. If you're experiencing an acute episode, or if you have severe back pain, you should not start the strategies in this book. It's important your GP refers you to a specialist. Alternatively, a physiotherapist might be able to help you settle your acute problems.

Putting it all together

The Physiocise method is designed to help you understand how your back pain may have arisen and what you can do to take control of your pain. This diagram sets out how the various components of the Physiocise framework fit together. Before you start to apply the principles and strategies, remember the typical activities in your day and how these also influence the stress on your back.

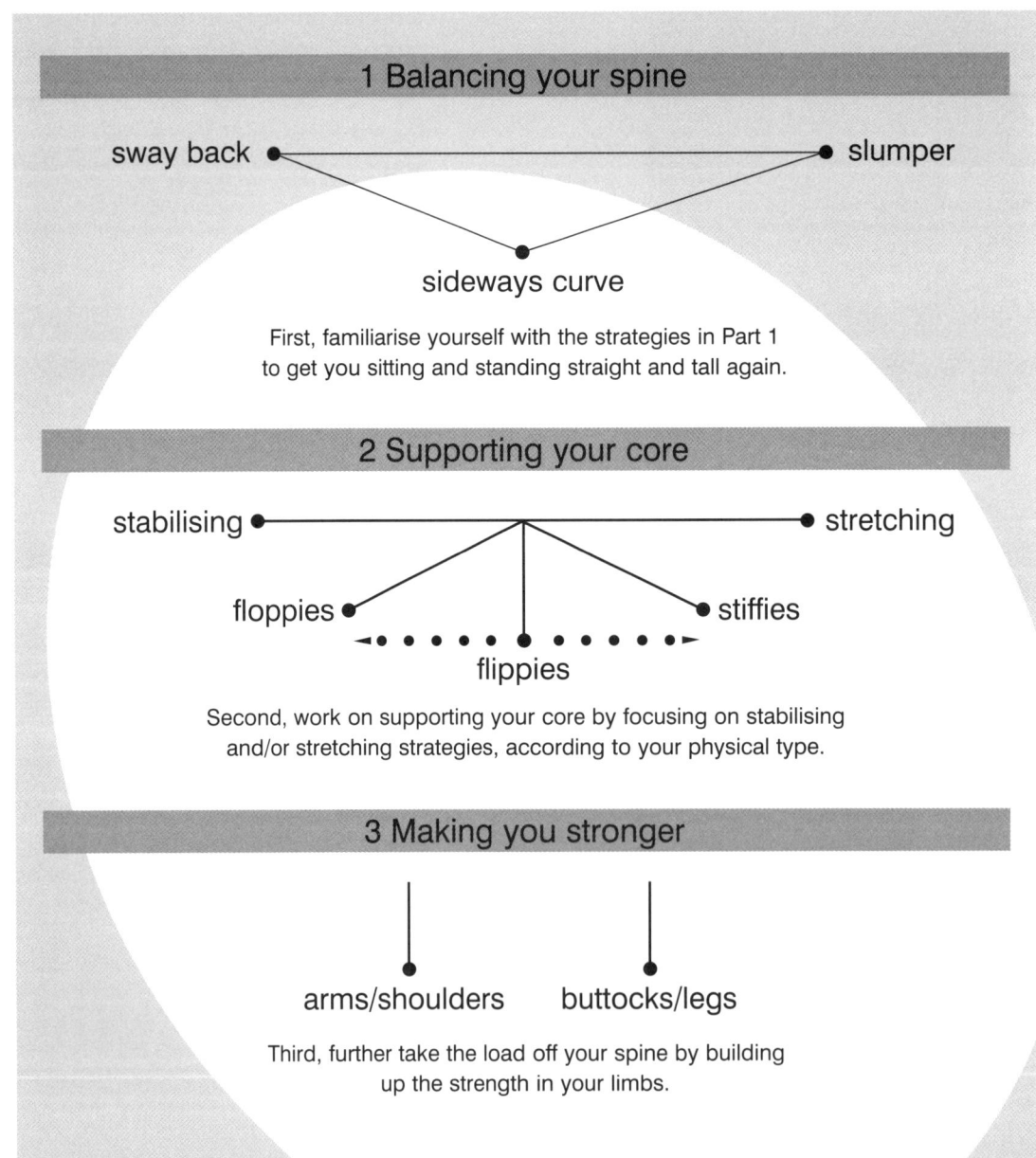

1 Balancing your spine

sway back — slumper

sideways curve

First, familiarise yourself with the strategies in Part 1
to get you sitting and standing straight and tall again.

2 Supporting your core

stabilising — stretching

floppies — stiffies

flippies

Second, work on supporting your core by focusing on stabilising
and/or stretching strategies, according to your physical type.

3 Making you stronger

arms/shoulders   buttocks/legs

Third, further take the load off your spine by building
up the strength in your limbs.

Equipment

It's important to get each strategy right to start with, otherwise you'll find that you don't improve.

In the initial stages you will need a few simple pieces of equipment to act as cues to remind you how to do the strategy perfectly and to help your brain work out where you are in space.

Your posture dots
Go to any newsagent and buy a roll of bright round stickers (about the size of a ten cent coin). These are invaluable to prompt your brain to find your perfect posture!

Your bottom clencher
This is a simple device I've developed to teach your buttock muscles to work properly again! Slip a credit card between the cheeks of your buttocks and hold it there for long periods to produce lovely firm buttocks.

A chair
You don't need a special chair, but it's helpful if it doesn't have arms or wheels. Later you can do the exercises on practically any chair, but to start with it's better not to slide around.

A wall, a bar and a full length mirror
These are used for your stretching exercises. The bar can be the railing of a fence or a balcony. Anything about 1.2 metres high that won't fall apart when you pull it, is ideal. Once you've got the stabilising and strengthening exercises in your brain, you'll be able to do them practically anywhere.

The mirror is helpful in the early stages of your program so that you can see how you move during an exercise. How you think you move and what it really looks like are often completely different.

The celebrity hibiscus kit
For this kit you'll need one plastic headband and a silk hibiscus (or similar flower) on a wire stem. This will help you focus on where your head is in relation to the rest of your body.

part one

Balancing your spine

Just as a car needs good wheel alignment to stop it developing uneven wear and tear on its tyres leading to more serious problems, so too your skeleton needs good alignment to stop uneven wear and tear on your joints.

The following strategies focus on keeping your alignment balanced and will help you find more efficient ways to sit, stand and walk.

The balancing strategies

Balancing your spine feels so good it will soon become something you do without thinking about it. We naturally want to repeat things that feel good and forget those that make us feel bad. Once you learn to balance your spine, you'll be able to sit for longer, stand comfortably in checkout queues and walk for longer without pain. After a while, not being balanced will actually feel worse.

Pain and aching are your body's alarm system. If you bend your wrist as far as it will go and hold it there with your other hand for a few seconds, it will quickly start to ache. When you release it, the pain won't go away immediately. The longer you've held your wrist, the longer the pain will take to go away.

Sitting or standing is a less extreme position for your joints, so the onset of pain is slower and more subtle. If you sit slumped at a desk for a few hours, after a while the ligaments which make up the joints in your back send messages to the brain that they've had enough. This is just a subtle background message, so often you'll just change your position slightly to take the load off – you might shift your bottom a bit, or uncross your legs. But because you're still slumped, the message to your brain becomes stronger and stronger until the ache becomes pain. Your brain is now very aware of that and wants the pain to stop. At this point you'll often consciously stand up to try to ease the load. You'll notice the pain doesn't go away immediately. The longer you've taken to recognise the warning messages, the longer the pain will take to subside.

The key to the balancing strategies is to use that subtle ache to remind you to re-balance your spine and take the load off, before you experience pain. By doing this you're teaching your brain and your muscles that being balanced feels good and slumping feels bad. Gradually your body will get better at keeping the good position instead of the bad.

Being balanced feels good. Slumping feels bad.

When you first start to work on your alignment strategies, you may find the posture dots and celebrity hibiscus useful resources. See page 31 for how to obtain them.

The posture dots

The posture dots are a simple and fun way to help you sit and stand straight. For example, sitting straight is not just about putting your shoulders back, it's about so many things that if you had to think of them all you wouldn't be able to think of anything else, let alone maintain the position! When you stick the posture dots on strategic places on your body, they function as physical clues to help you find the right balance position without much thought.

Initially use them in front of a mirror to help you practise and focus. After a while you won't need to actually wear them as imagining them will give you a simple point of reference.

Also, try placing some posture dots in a few, highly visible positions around the house, such as the handle of the fridge, on the kitchen tap, the bathroom mirror, the front of the computer and the back of the front door. Every time you see them they'll give you a subtle reminder about your posture!

The celebrity hibiscus

The secret to keeping your spine balanced is understanding how to keep your centre core relatively still while the limbs move.

If you watched the 400 metre races and middle distance races during the Sydney Olympics, you would have noticed that the runners who were going to win were the ones who could keep their form to the end. As runners fatigued you could see their head start to sway and their body move from side to side, instead of their core staying stable and their arms and legs being the only moving elements.

The celebrity hibiscus will help you feel where your head is in space. If your head is centred, your trunk will also be centred and balanced. If your head is dropped to one side, your trunk will compensate. Like the posture dots, you only need to use the hibiscus in the early stages to focus your brain, then you'll be able to just imagine it is there.

The sitting posture dots

Equipment
- chair
- 3 posture dots
- mirror

Starting position
- Position your chair in front of a mirror.

- Find the boniest point at the front of your breastbone and walk your fingers down until you feel a gap. Put a posture dot at that point. Called the "centre dot", this will become your most important dot.

- Next find the boniest point at the front of your shoulder and put a dot there.

- Do the same on the other shoulder. Your dots should form a triangle.

widen the distance
between your centre dot
and your belly button

The movement

● Put the little finger of your right hand in your belly button and your thumb on your centre dot.

● Slump! The distance between your thumb and your little finger will narrow.

● Now lift your abdomen and widen the space between your fingers, being careful not to arch your back, until the centre dot is facing straight ahead.

● Now slump again – you'll probably feel your stomach spread as well.

● Lift your dots and the stomach will suck in automatically.

The result

● When your centre dot drops, your shoulders roll forward, your chin pokes out and your chest drops.

● When you lift your centre dot, your shoulders drop back and down, your chin tucks in and, voila, perfect posture!

Try this

● Slump and let your dots drop.

● Now try and pull your shoulders back.

This action is almost impossible, yet it's what most people do when they try to sit up straight. They pull their shoulders back but don't lift their chests. This makes it mechanically too hard, so they collapse again. Lifting the centre dot is crucial to balancing the upper part of your torso when seated.

Balancing your bottom bones – BBB

Equipment
● chair
● mirror

Balancing your bottom bones (BBB)
is another simple way to balance
your spine and improve your posture.
While the sitting posture dots strategy
aligns the upper part of your torso,
balancing your bottom bones aligns the
lower part. You may feel tired and achy
at first because your stabilising muscles
aren't yet able to hold you for long periods,
but after three weeks or so the aching
will gradually stop as your muscles
and joints grow stronger in this position.

Starting position
● Always sit on the edge of your chair.

● To find your bottom bones, place your
hands under your buttocks and feel for
two hard bones.

● Put your feet at least 60 centimetres
apart, more if you have long legs.

● Now put your hands on your hip
bones just below your waist,
thumbs facing backwards.

gentle curve
in lower back

lower back
too swayed

tummy popping out

Lift your dots then balance your bottom bones.

tummy in

The movement
● Slump by letting your bottom bones roll under. Your chest will drop, your stomach will spread and your chest will be squashed.

● Now gently roll your bottom bones back by arching your back as far as it can go

● Slump again and feel your bottom bones roll under. Then arch your back as far as you can go.

● Now find the middle point between these two positions. This is the point at which your bottom bones are balanced, making it easy to hold up your spine.

The result
● Your chest lifts and at the same time your posture straightens – you'll be 15 cm taller.

Try this
● Repeat the movement with knees together, then with your legs together. Now try with your legs crossed

Trying to BBB with your legs together is hard work and trying to BBB with your legs crossed is almost impossible! Always sit with your legs slightly apart to make it easy to BBB.

Sitting celebrity hibiscus

Equipment
- celebrity hibiscus
- chair
- mirror

Once you can lift your dots and BBB, the final step in efficient sitting posture is the position of your head. This strategy helps you maintain your head position.

Starting position
- Attach the flower to the headband as shown so that the stamen of the hibiscus is pointing forward like a trumpet. Put it on your head.

- Attach your posture dots.

- Sit on the edge of the chair facing the mirror. Now slump!

- Your hibiscus will drop as your centre dot drops, your chin comes forward and your stomach spreads.

Don't forget your head position!

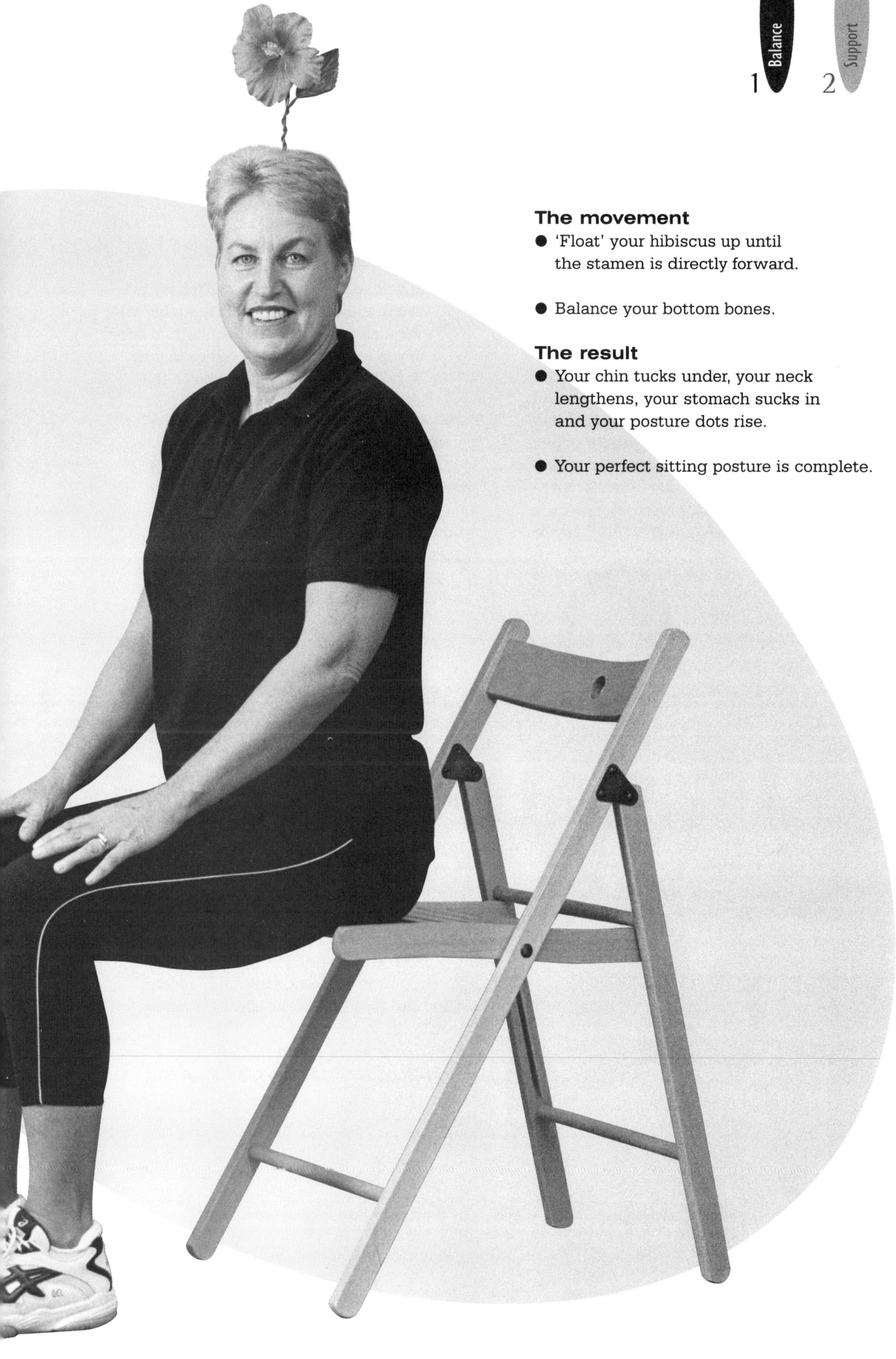

The movement

- 'Float' your hibiscus up until the stamen is directly forward.

- Balance your bottom bones.

The result

- Your chin tucks under, your neck lengthens, your stomach sucks in and your posture dots rise.

- Your perfect sitting posture is complete.

Sitting with one leg in front

Equipment
● chair

Here is another simple way to balance
your spine when you sit.

Starting position
● Sit on the edge of your chair.

● Put one leg in front of you and
the other slightly under the chair.

The movement
● BBB and lift your dots.

● If you have a chair that adjusts, try to
angle the seat down slightly so that it's
even easier to balance your bottom bones.
If you have a chair with legs, put your
legs in position, then balance on the
front two legs of the chair only.

The result
● Your spine is beautifully balanced.

Sit on the chair's

More balanced sitting strategies

Sitting in cars

Long distance driving can be hard on your back and neck. When you get into your car, check you're well balanced by doing the following:

- Wiggle your bottom back into the seat, but not so you're arching your lower back.

- Lift your bottom slightly off the seat and then put it down again to make sure you're sitting evenly on both bottom bones.

- Lift your posture dots.

- Now adjust your rear vision mirror so you can see well when in this position.

- If at any point you can no longer see out of your rear vision mirror, you have dropped your dots. This will round your shoulders and your neck, increasing tension on your spine. Re-check your bottom bone position every so often and make sure it hasn't slipped forward.

- Take regular breaks and listen to your back. If you're getting grumbly aches, get out and stretch before they turn into pain

Forget expensive ergonomic furniture

For many years we've relied on ergonomic furniture, lumbar supports and expensive chairs to improve sitting posture. To maintain efficient sitting posture all the time, not just when you're in those chairs, it's important to change your habits, rather than your environment. In this way your muscles learn to hold you up, not external props.

- Sit on the edge of the chair and use your own muscles to hold you there. Even if you have an adjustable chair, still sit on the edge but try to adjust the front of the seat so that it angles down slightly. Stools make BBB even easier. Try to keep your elbows off the table or the desk as this encourages you to slump and use your arms to prop you up instead of your trunk muscles.

- Expect to have some increase in discomfort for the first three to five weeks as your back gets used to these new positions. It's like starting a new fitness regime – you would expect to wake up a bit sore and sorry for the first few weeks as your body gets used to the new demands. But if the discomfort concerns you, see your doctor or physiotherapist.

The standing posture dots - step 1

Equipment
- posture dots
- mirror

Starting position
- Attach your posture dots.

- Stand in front of the mirror.

- Make sure your weight is even on both legs and your feet are parallel.

dots rolling forward

rounded shoulders

Stand tall

broad shoulders

long neck

The movement

- Put the little finger of your right hand on your belly button and your thumb on your centre dot.

- Slump.

- Your stomach will spread, your shoulders roll forward and your chin poke out. This may well be a familiar sight!

- Now stand side-on and look at your posture.

- Widen the space between your fingers until the centre dot is facing straight ahead, but don't overarch your lower back.

The result

- Your shoulders roll back, your neck lengthens, your stomach sucks in and your head lifts up.

lift your dots

The standing posture dots - step 2

Equipment
- posture dots
- mirror

This strategy is particularly good for helping slumpers and sway backs keep themselves upright without overcompensating. Sometimes just lifting your dots isn't enough, you also need to think about where those dots are in relation to your hips.

Starting position
- Create your posture dot triangle.

- Stand side-on to a mirror.

- Place the index finger of one hand on your centre dot. With the other hand, move your index finger below your belly button until you feel bone (your pubic bone).

The movement
- Slump. Your centre dot will drop behind the line of your pubic bone, your lower back will sway and your bottom roll forward.

- Now lift your centre dot away from your belly button without overarching your lower back.

- Keep your centre dot in an imaginary line over your pubic bone.

The result
- Your back straightens, your shoulders drop down and you're no longer overcompensating.

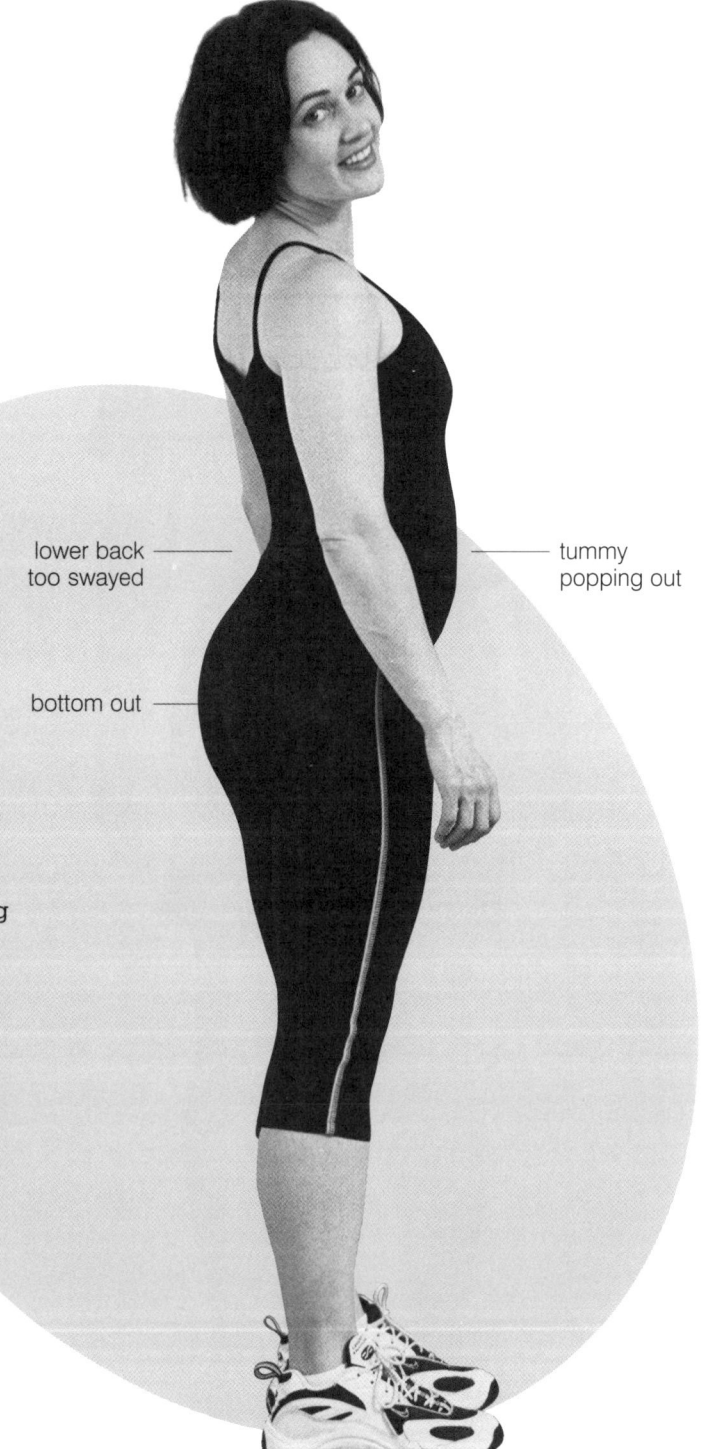

lower back too swayed

tummy popping out

bottom out

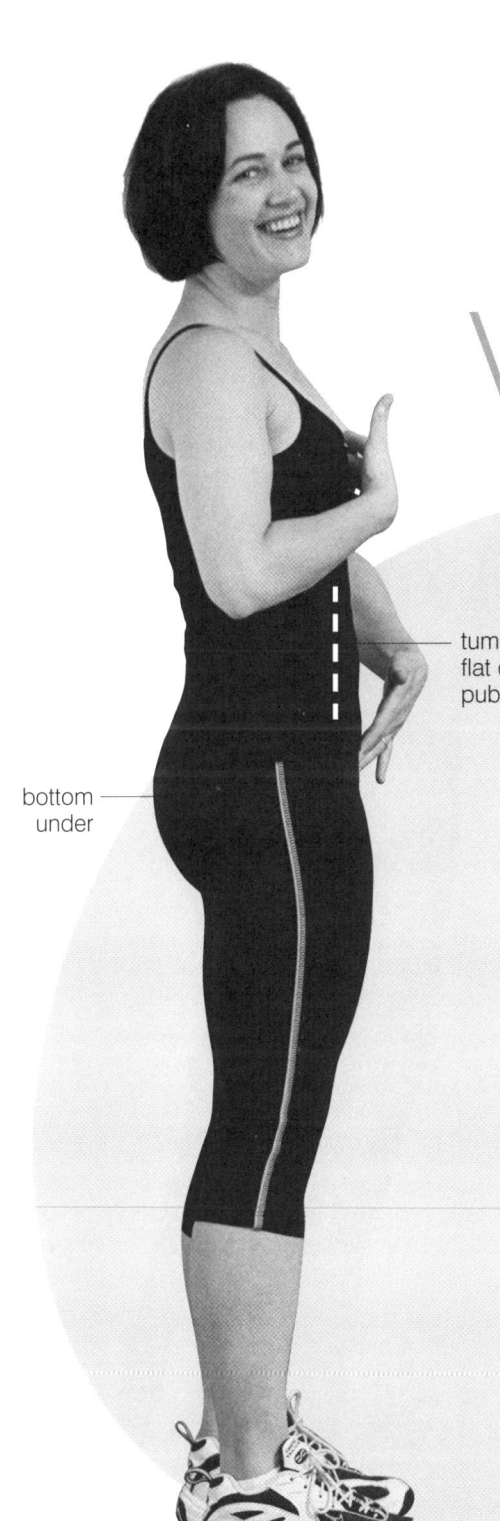

tummy
flat over
pubic bone

bottom
under

When you align all the sections of your spine standing tall is easy!

Sloppy standing

Many people stand with their weight
on one leg, and their feet rotated out
at various angles. This puts uneven
pressure on the spine and can switch
off the deep stabilising system. The more
you slop when you stand, the harder
it is for your muscles to hold you up.
The way you position
your feet will also
change the position
of your whole body.

Don't rotate your feet when you stand.

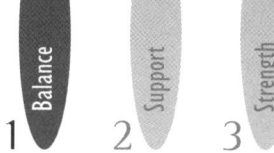

Straight standing

Always stand evenly on both feet, with your feet parallel as if you were standing on skis. This will balance you from the ground up. If you start on an even base, it's much easier to keep the rest of your spine balanced and the forces even. You don't have to be perfectly balanced all the time, just try and catch yourself when you slip into a sloppy stance.

Balance from the ground up.

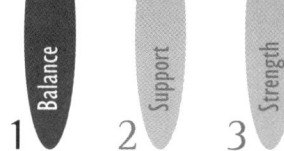

Standing for a long time

Equipment
- small step or low ledge

If you've tried everything else – you've stood evenly, you've lifted your dots and you've put your centre dot over your pubic bone – but you still ache, your lower back corset is fatigued. You need to take the load off your back.

This strategy is a great way to relax your lower back if you have to stand for a long time.

Starting position
- Put your foot on the step or ledge, making sure it's not too high.

The movement
- Now rest your foot so that it takes the weight off your spine. Make sure you don't let the hip above your straight leg drop.

- Swap your feet every so often.

The result
- Your lower back is relaxed.

More balanced standing strategies

Socialising

The pub is one place where people spend long periods sitting or standing. Pub furniture has evolved to help people stay comfortable. The foot ledge on bar stools provides just the support we need to take the load off our backs and stay there for hours. The bar stool itself is high, allowing us to balance our bottoms without realising it. Unfortunately, all this good posture falls apart if you end up slumped on the bar!

At home

Many women who spend a lot of time at home maintaining houses and families rarely have time to sit, often spending a great deal of time standing in the kitchen. Protect your back by keeping a low stool (about 20 to 30 cm high and available from most hardware shops) in the kitchen. The lightweight plastic versions designed as a step for children at sinks are also useful. Whether you're peeling potatoes, chopping, standing while speaking on the phone or washing up, put one foot on the stool every now and then to take the load off your back and give it a break. Be careful not to rely on this all the time, and only after you've used your other standing strategies first as they are better for activating your muscles.

Feeling down

The way you feel can profoundly affect your posture.

It's important to see aches for what they are – sometimes the physical symptoms of an unhappy situation. If you feel you need to speak to someone about this, there are many excellent councillors and psychologists your doctor could recommend. These specialists will be able to guide you through dealing with the possible emotional causes of your aches and pains.

Breasts

The posture of many women is influenced by the size of their breasts. Some women spend years rounding their shoulders because they feel their breasts are too big; others do the same because they believe their breasts are too small.

Standing and sitting straight is not about poking out your breasts. By lifting your posture dots you're not pushing your breasts out, just up and away from your belly button. It also helps to wear a good bra – it's amazing how often old, loose bras contribute to neck pain because you lift your shoulders to try to keep the bra straps up.

Walking celebrity hibiscus

Equipment
- celebrity hibiscus
- posture dots

If your neck corset keeps the position of your head in place, preventing it from moving from side to side, you'll be able to maintain the lower back corset as the head lined up with the trunk keeps it stable. The hibiscus headband allows you to think about the position of your head when you sit or stand and, more importantly, when you walk or run.

Learning to maintain your deep corsets when you sit and stand is one thing, but to keep them in place when you walk or run is more difficult. Using your celebrity hibiscus will help enormously.

Starting position
- Put on your hibiscus headband and attach your posture dots.

- Stand in front of a mirror.

- Now slump. Your hibiscus will drop, along with your centre dot, and your stomach will spread.

The movement
- 'Float' your hibiscus up. As you lift your hibiscus, your posture dots will rise and your stomach go in.

- Now move back from the mirror as far away as possible so that you can see yourself walking towards it.

- As you walk forward, keep your hibiscus up and still – your head and body will line up and keep your body stable. Swing your arms, but don't let your hibiscus move from side to side. Initially it's easy to keep your hibiscus still and up, but as you get tired it starts to drop and flop around.

The result
- Your head is in line with your trunk and balanced between your shoulders.

- This has the effect of switching on your deep neck corset and your lower back corset, keeping your trunk stable.

Keep your hibiscus up to help switch on your deep muscle corsets.

head aligned

neck corset activated

lower back corset activated

How NOT to carry

Carrying badly is something we all do sometimes when the demands of our day make it seem impossible to do otherwise. Too many shopping bags at once to avoid an extra trip back to the car, juggling a baby, a handbag and a phone, carrying a heavy laptop *and* a suitcase are all examples of bad carrying habits. For the sake of better alignment, it's important to learn a few simple tips to make carrying less of a strain on our spines.

heavy bag straps on shoulders lead to neck pain

leaning down leads to lower back pain

shoulders leaning forwards places more load on the neck

cradling a phone pinches the neck joints

always carrying on one side leads to muscle imbalance

using fingers only to carry places more load on the shoulders and neck

keeping the weight all on one leg places increased pressure on the spine

How to carry

Most people use one side more than the other to carry, usually with the non-dominant hand so that their dominant hand is left free to do the finer things, such as using keys to open doors. Become aware of which side you favour to carry heavy items, then swap every once in a while.

Women who have a slight scoliosis, making one shoulder higher than the other, usually carry their shoulder bag on their high shoulder to stop it slipping off. If you fall into this group, don't carry shoulder bags at all. Always carry things under the arm of the high shoulder to help straighten up the back.

Avoid carrying heavy computer cases or luggage on your shoulder when travelling. Instead, strap bags on lightweight sets of wheels. This makes luggage more portable and leaves your shoulders weight-free.

When carrying a child, swap him or her from side to side. Easing the back pain of a mother with toddlers often requires nothing more than having her stop carrying a child always on the one hip.

When carrying a heavy briefcase or shopping bags, always bend your elbows. This distributes the load through your arm instead of putting it all on your neck.

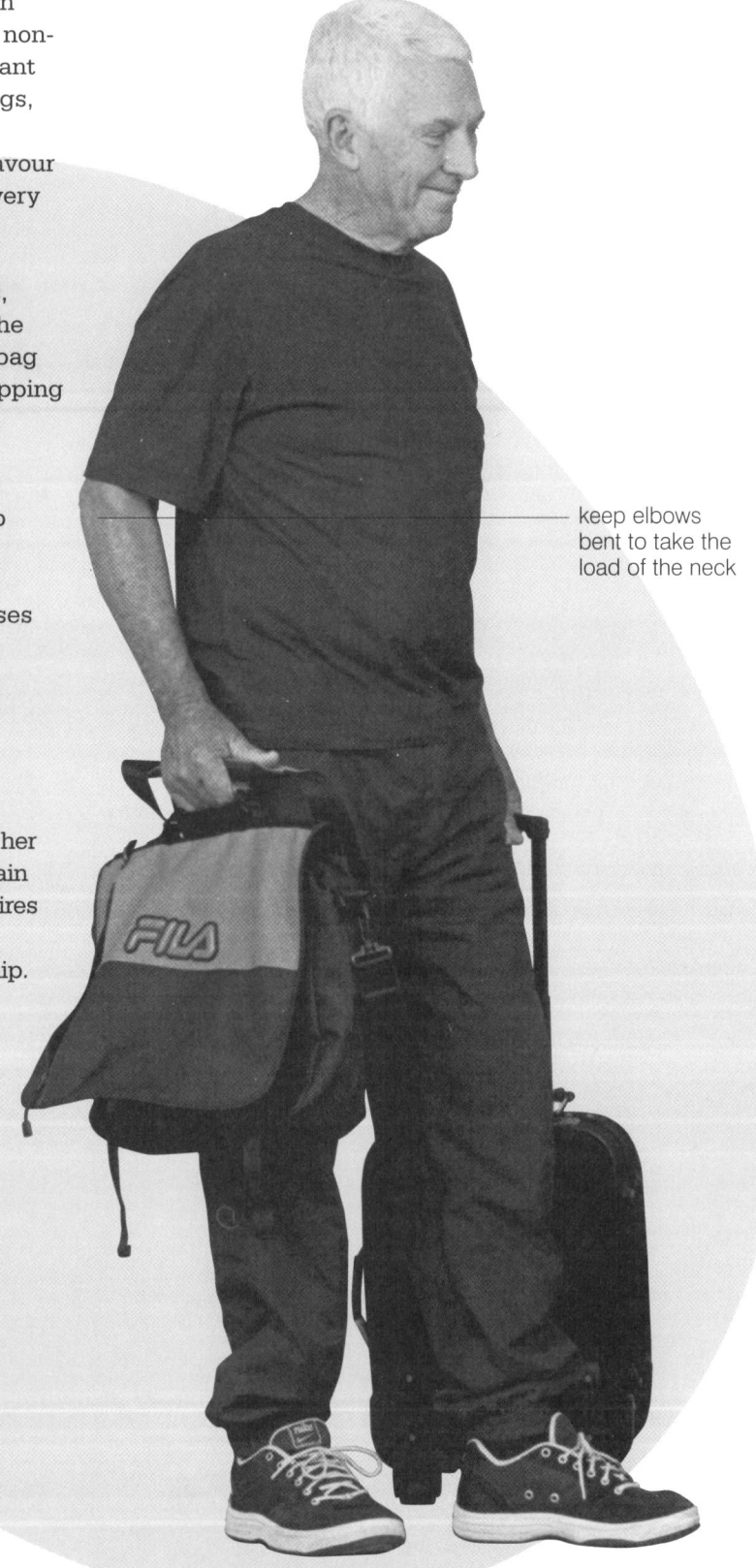

keep elbows bent to take the load of the neck

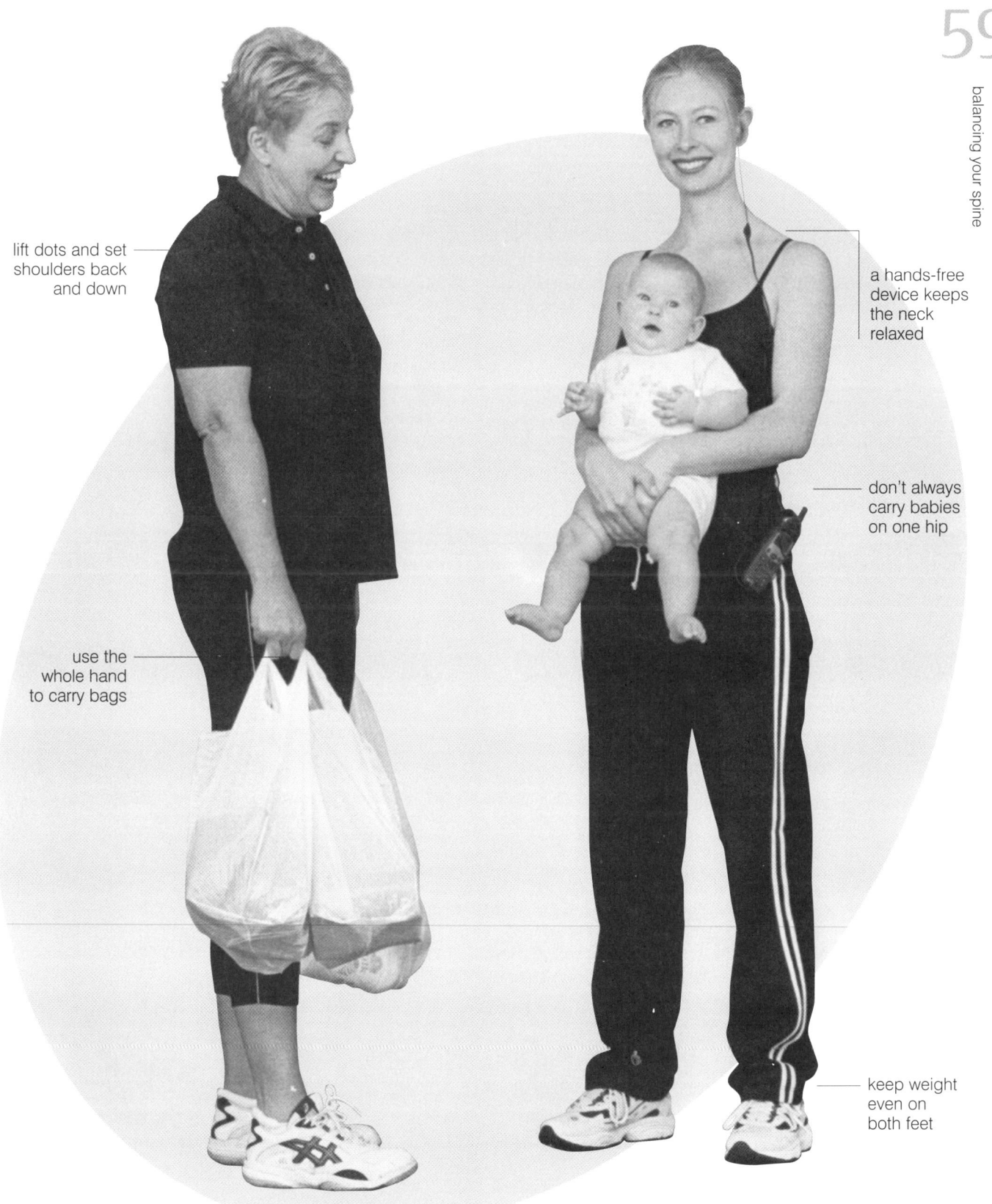

lift dots and set
shoulders back
and down

a hands-free
device keeps
the neck
relaxed

don't always
carry babies
on one hip

use the
whole hand
to carry bags

keep weight
even on
both feet

How NOT to lift

Lifting poorly is a classic way to injure your back or aggravate existing pain. Once again, a few simple tips can help to maintain good alignment and minimise the risk of injury.

Always bend your knees when lifting.

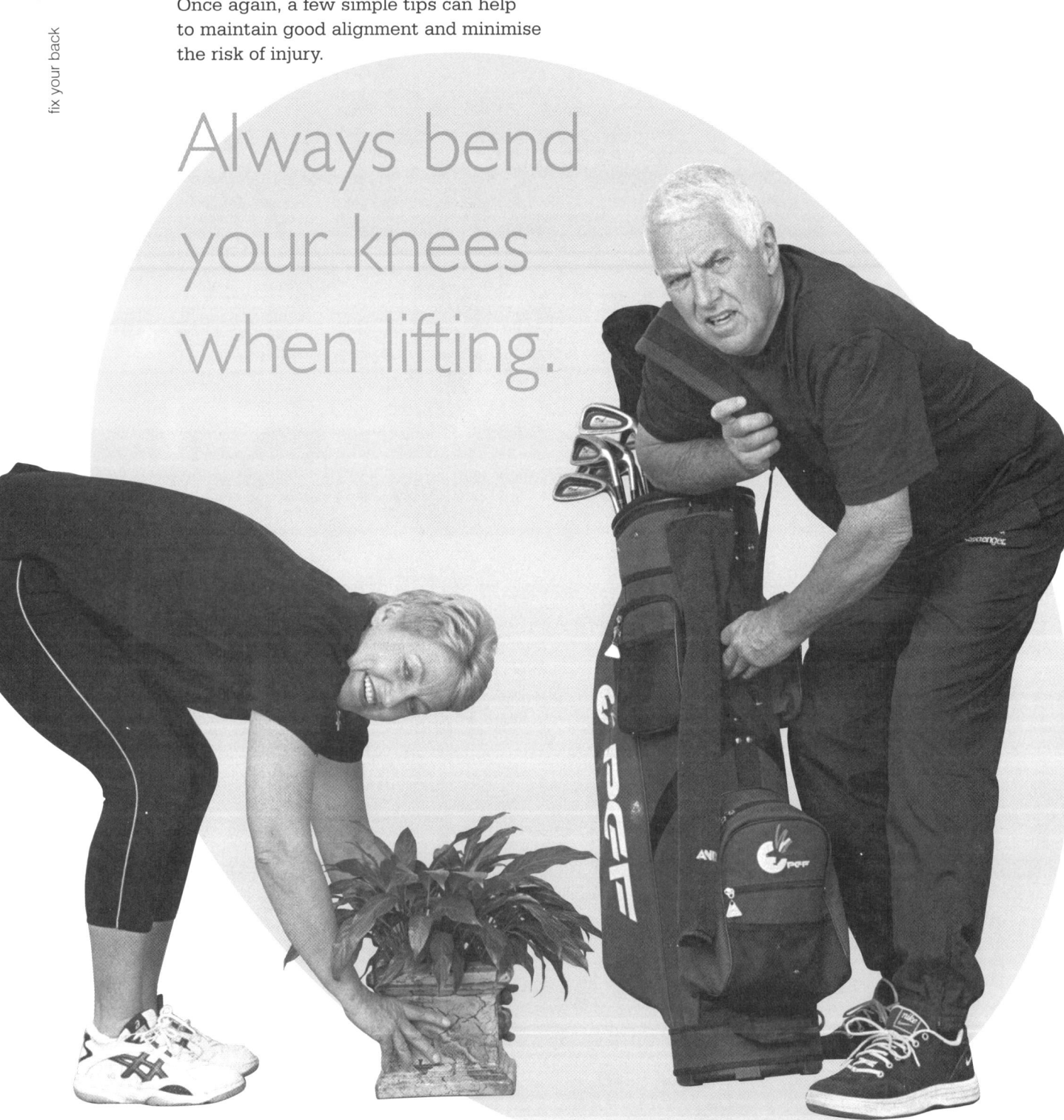

How to lift

- Bend your knees.
- Bring the object close to your body.
- Bend your elbows.
- Brace your abdominal muscles
  to protect your lower back.

And think about what you're doing.

Balancing the professional athlete

For most of us mere mortals, keeping our spines balanced is the equivalent of keeping good wheel alignment in the standard family car. Now imagine a professional athlete.

Instead of the family car, they're driving a Ferrari. Every subtle problem with alignment, balance, power and speed is critical to highest level performance.

If you're a professional sportsperson you're required to push your body to its limits. You need to function at peak levels, train and perform, often without the breaks that used to occur in the days of non-professional sport. Your biggest fear is usually injury, the most difficult to overcome being overuse injuries.

Overuse injuries have many causes, including excessive training and shoe or equipment changes. Overwhelmingly, many overuse injuries are the result of muscles trying to compensate for jobs they shouldn't really be doing. One of the reasons for this is faulty alignment. Gradually these muscles start to break down as they were never really designed for that job, resulting in overuse injury.

To prevent injury it's critical to balance your spine. Whether you're a rugby player, golfer, gymnast or swimmer, your body needs to be perfectly balanced.

Balancing the everyday exerciser

You may not be a professional athlete, but you're someone who loves to exercise.

So it can be frustrating when exercise seems to cause problems and pain – golfers with bad backs, social runners with achilles tendonitis or regular gym goers with shoulder problems. After all, isn't exercise meant to be good for you?

Just like the professional athlete, if you're pushing your body that little bit further and harder, any subtle alignment problems will start to cause pain. Even if the problem seems to be in a specific area (such as a foot or knee) it's often in fact the result of compensations for imbalance and poor stability in the trunk.

If you think this may be part of your problem, start with the alignment hints and try to balance your spine as well as you can. Then you can start working on other things that might be stopping you, like tight or weak muscles.

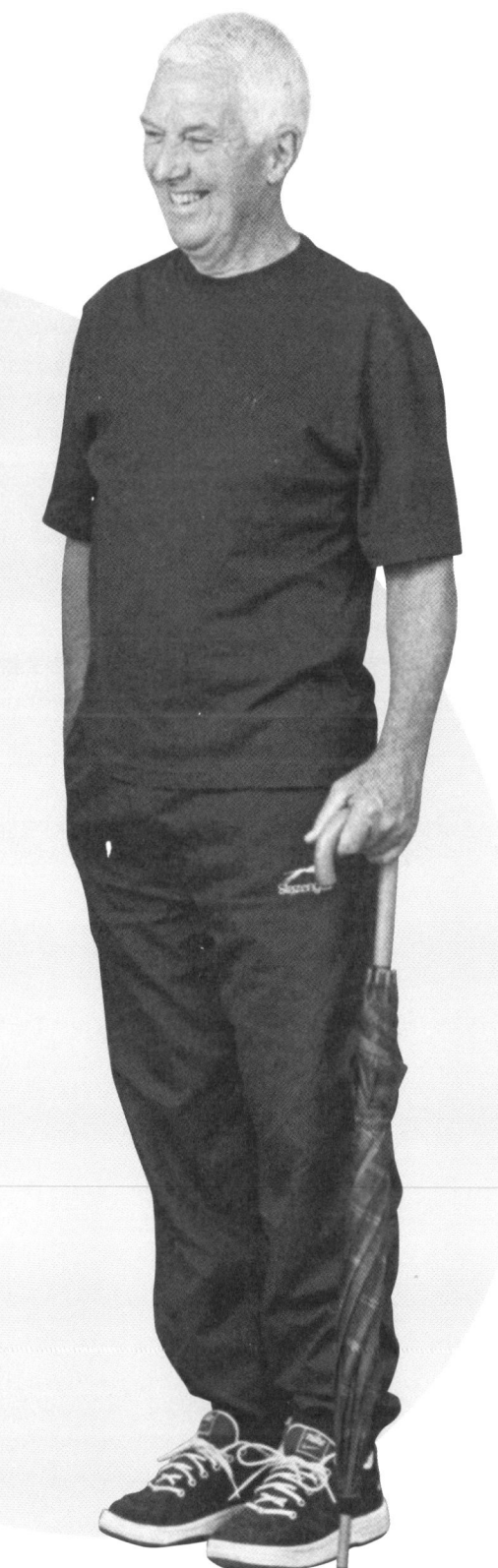

Balancing children

Unfortunately, we are seeing an increase in the incidence of backache, headaches and neck problems in young people and children. Just as in adult back pain, much of this is the product of a combination of poor posture and weak muscles due to long hours of sitting coupled with less general activity. A great deal of school-age children's learning now takes place sitting at a desk and more and more of their leisure is technology-based in the form of computers, TV's and the like. Consequently, they no longer have the chances to develop the strong postural muscles to take them through their lives.

Primary school children

The scourge of good posture in primary age children is the craze for nintendos, gameboys and computers. There are a few simple things you can do to try to minimise the effect on their posture:

● Limit the amount of time they use computers and electronic games. Aim for short periods followed by outdoor activity to balance the sitting.

● Get them to lift the gameboy screen to their face rather than leaving it in their lap and bringing their face down to it. This will keep their spines straighter and is less stressful on their necks.

● Children generally like the 'lift your dots' message and can usually be easily reminded to balance when they sit, at desks and in front of computers. Try sticking some dots on the computer screen as a reminder.

● Encourage climbing, hanging from ropes and outdoor activities as much as possible.

Children need to use this time in their lives to develop not only their alignment but also their deep muscle strength. If they don't have it at 8 years old it will be very hard to find it at 28.

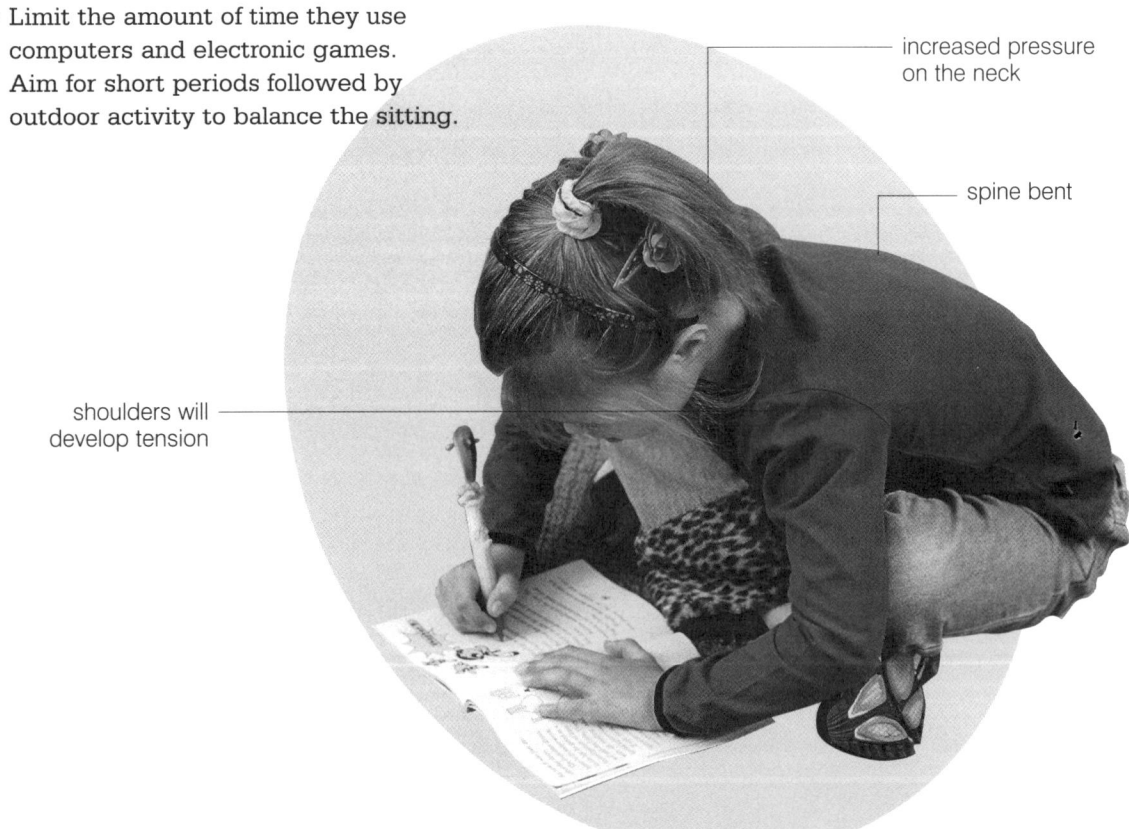

increased pressure on the neck

spine bent

shoulders will develop tension

Teenagers

Changing a teenager's posture is a daunting job – how much poor posture is due to muscle imbalance and how much to attitude? The attitude component is significant. If it is maintained long enough, there is the risk that the bad posture will become entrenched and fixing it will become more difficult.

Asking a teenager, who already feels unsure of their place in the world to lift their dots and stand tall is often met with the most withering of looks. Much as the despairing parent wants to stop the problem turning into the same one that they themselves have struggled with for years, the teenage mind rarely anticipates the future. While it may seem a losing battle, there are a few things you can do while you wait for their attitude to change:

● Never let teenagers study sitting on the bed or on floors.

● Always try to get them to eat dinner at a table without their elbows holding them up.

● At the end of the day, encourage them to lie on the floor face up with a cushion between their neck and their waist while watching TV to straighten out the slumping tendencies of the day. They will only be able to do this for a few minutes at a time, but if they persist it will really help. Then they can flip over and lie on their tummies, propped up on their elbows, for a while. The purpose of this is to try to keep the spine out of the slumped position.

● Don't let them carry school bags on one shoulder, and try to minimise the number of books they take to and from school (although this is often tricky.)

● Encourage backstroke swimming rather than freestyle as this helps develop the muscles needed to hold them straight, rather than the ones that pull them forward.

● Encourage physical activity – any physical activity is good activity.

● Keep a good sense of humour!

neck relaxed

back straight
and tummy on

part two

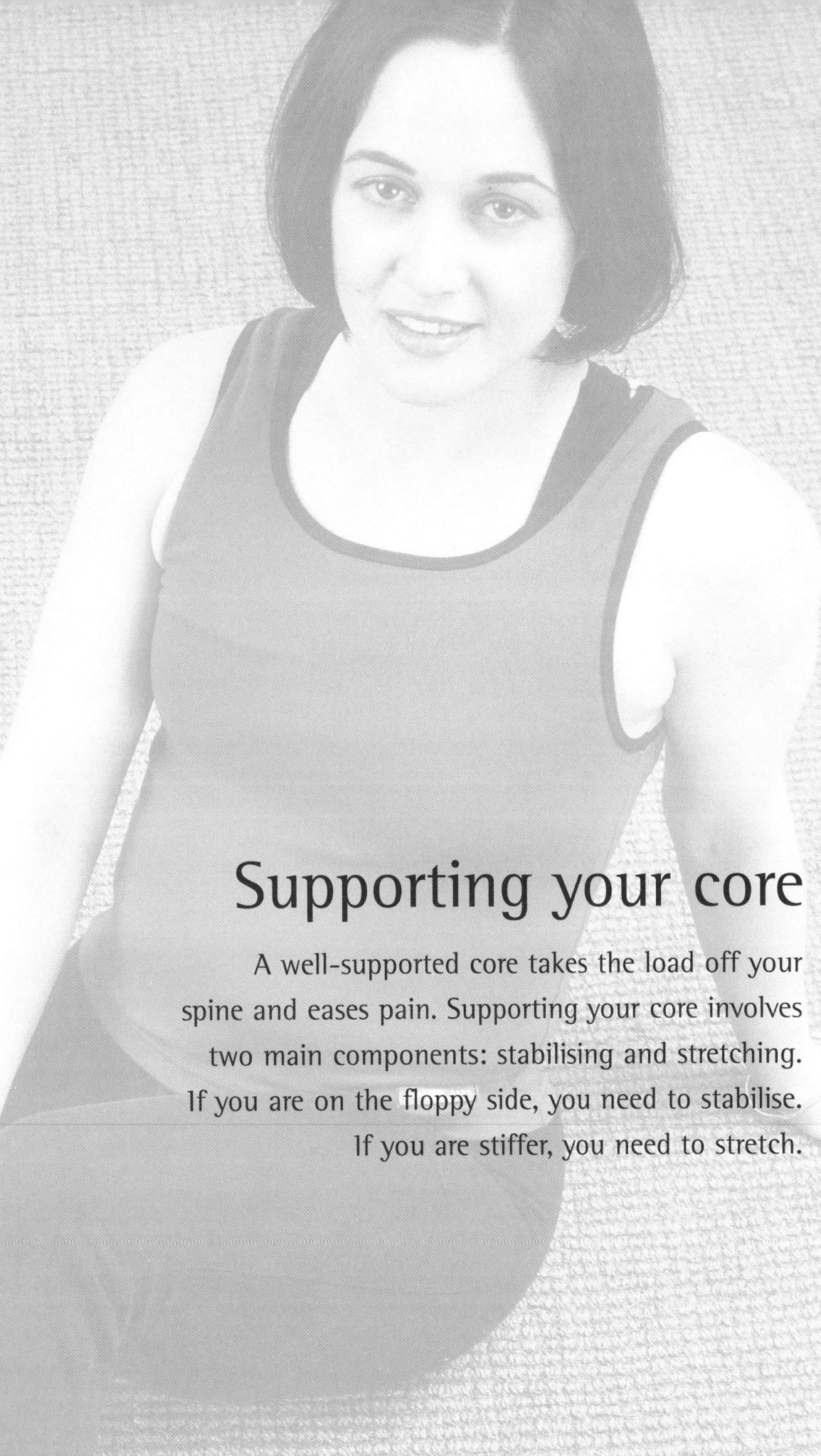

Supporting your core

A well-supported core takes the load off your spine and eases pain. Supporting your core involves two main components: stabilising and stretching. If you are on the floppy side, you need to stabilise. If you are stiffer, you need to stretch.

Wobbly bits and stiff bits

Our spines have four main sections – two are primarily
'moving sections' and two 'loading'.

The two 'moving' sections are the neck
and the lower back, designed to allow
us to twist, turn, bend and straighten.
The two loading sections, the thoracic
spine (with the ribcage which wraps
around from front to back) and the pelvis
(which helps support the base of the
spine) are designed to be supporting
structures for the spine as well as the
limbs. Because they have many bones
joining them from the front and sides,
they also generally have less movement
and are inherently more stable.

The 'moving' bits, the neck and the lower
back, don't have many bones around them
to provide a structural support. This is
what gives these areas enormous freedom
of movement. They rely on two muscular
corsets at the front and sides to support,
or stabilise, the spine at the back. The one
that is more important to focus on here is
the lower back.

Relying on muscles for stability rather
than bony support also makes these areas
more vulnerable than the loading sections.
Moving parts generally wear out more
easily and are more susceptible to
breaking down. This is why there's a high
incidence of injury to the spinal structures
themselves –the discs, ligaments and
joints of the lower back and neck areas.

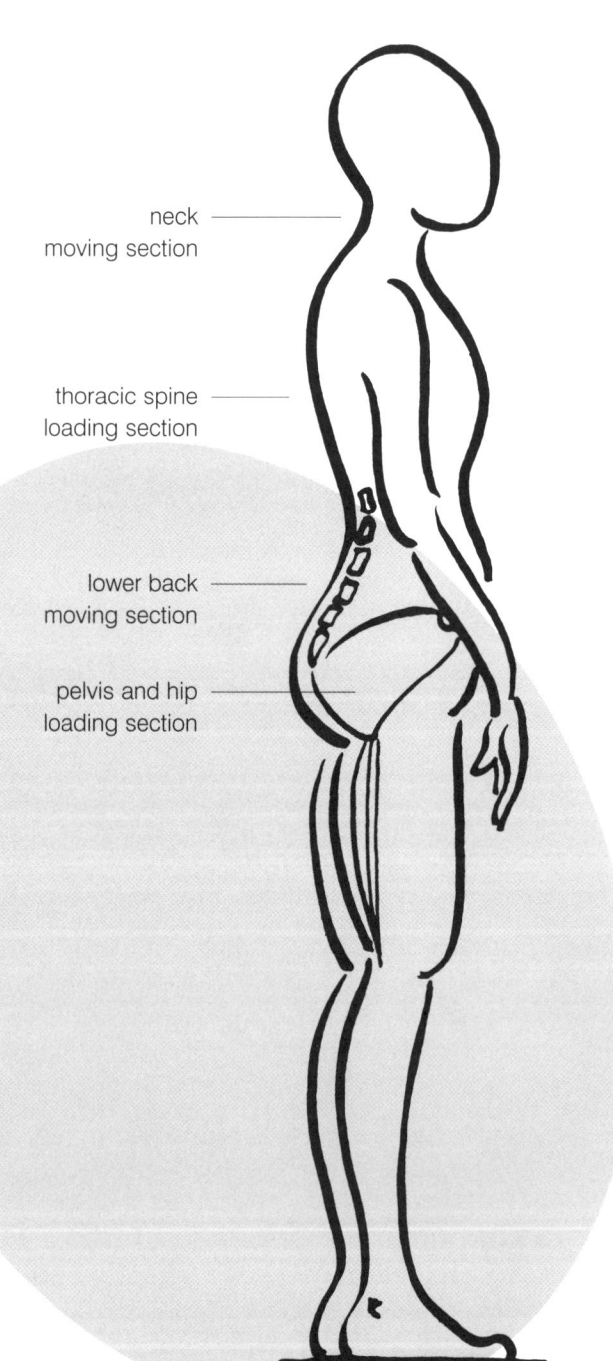

neck
moving section

thoracic spine
loading section

lower back
moving section

pelvis and hip
loading section

In a balanced spine, the loading areas support and the moving areas move.

If you're a stiffy your spine has always been a little stiff anyway, which means the back of your lower back corset actually has a little more bony support. This in turn means you don't rely on your muscles quite as much to give you stability in your lower back. Although you have less movement, and your muscles look weak, you also probably have less pain. Your priority is stretching your stiff bits. The stretching strategies are ideal for increasing your movement. Stabilising your core is still important, but not your priority.

If you're on the floppy side, your spine and the bones, joints and ligaments of the lower back are already flexible. Your spine has a limited ability to support itself without the help of its muscles. Any problem that weakens either the neck or lower back corset can have serious long-term effects, often resulting in a great deal of pain. The only way to fix your back for good is to re-establish the stability of your muscular corsets, particularly the one in the lower back, to take the load off your spine. Your priority is the stabilising strategies. You can stretch as much as you like, but it will only bring temporary relief. In some cases, stretching can make you feel worse because you are making your spine even more unstable.

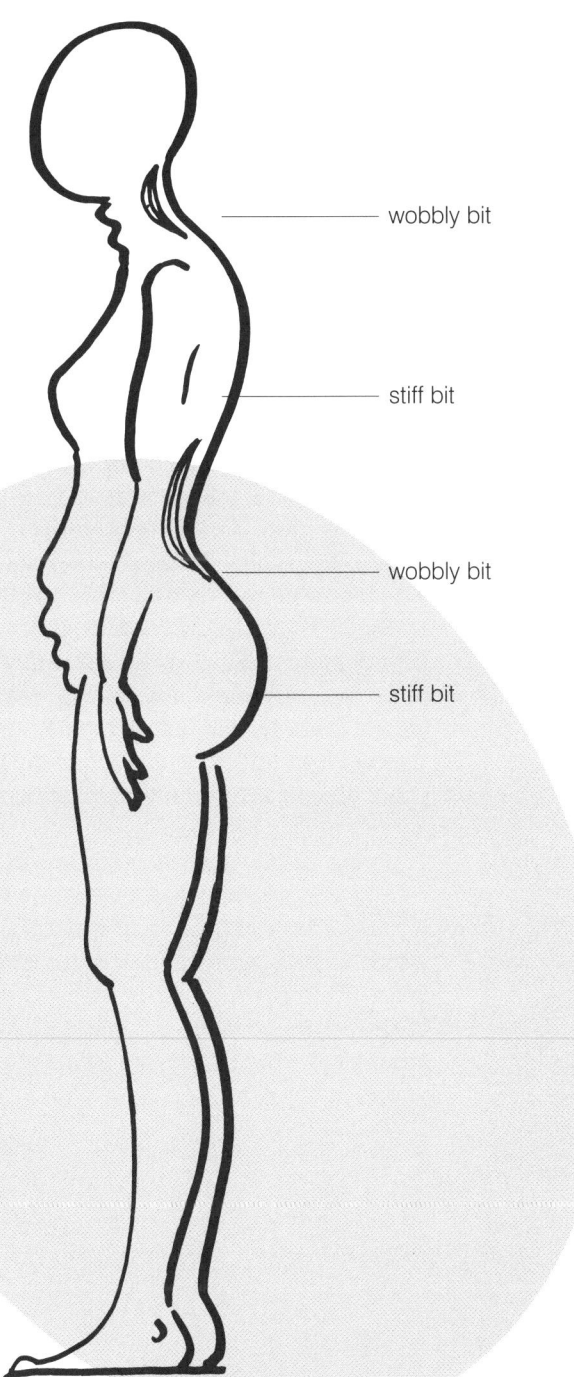

wobbly bit

stiff bit

wobbly bit

stiff bit

The lower back corset

The lower back corset is made up of several sets of interweaving muscles that work together to support the spine and hold us upright.

The front and side walls are the muscles of the stomach, which wrap around horizontally to join the muscles of the lower back. The back muscles and the stomach muscles work together as a unit. They look a bit like the corsets your grandmother might have worn. The stomach muscles are arranged in layers. To have a truly stable corset you need to understand what each layer does, and target the most important ones individually.

The corset also has a lid and a floor that play a vital role in its total stability. The lid is formed by the **diaphragm** at the base of the lungs. When the diaphragm is working efficiently as part of the whole corset, it allows you to breath and keep your corset working at the same time. Once you have good control over the lid of your corset, you can use it to help activate the walls and floor. Without this ability you'll always struggle with your tummy.

The base of the corset is made up of a sling of muscles called the **pelvic floor**. If these are weak and keep dropping away, much of the stability of the sides is lost. To have your entire corset working at maximum capacity you need to strengthen your pelvic floor. This applies equally to men and women.

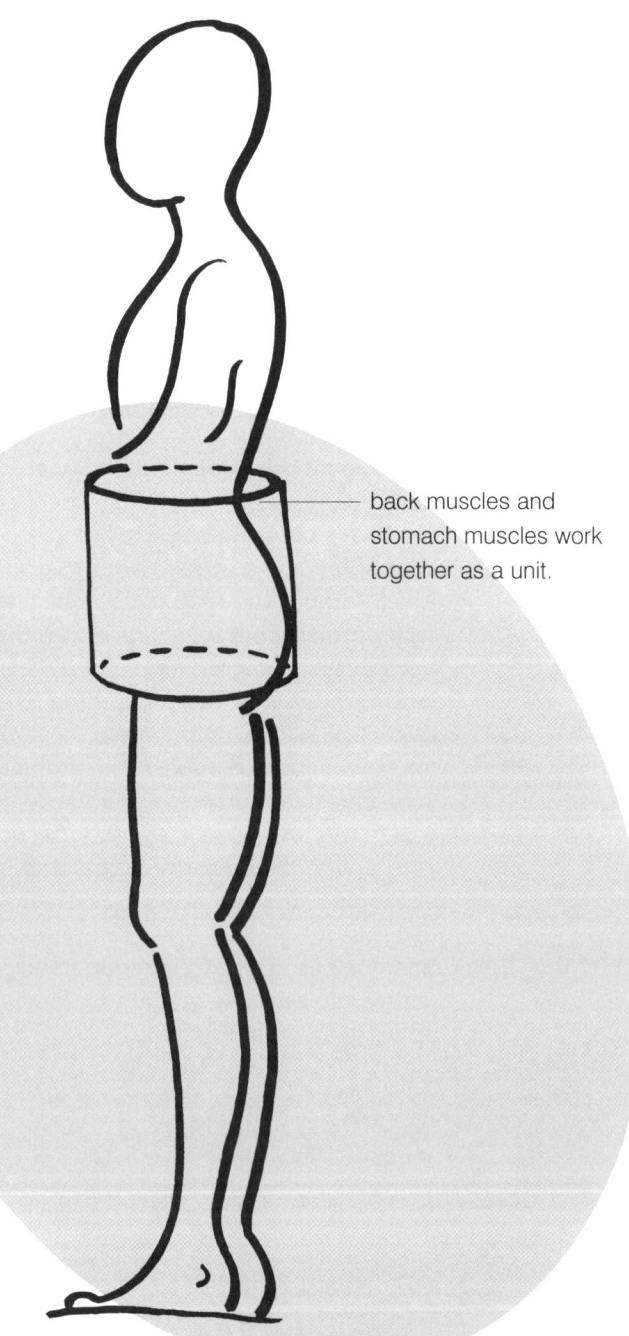

back muscles and stomach muscles work together as a unit.

Just as weakness in one part of the corset affects all the other parts, so building endurance in one part helps build endurance in the rest of it.

When you think about all those muscles that need to work efficiently in unison to provide a stable, supported, pain-free spine you begin to have some understanding of the potential for back injury. It starts to become clearer why everyone you know seems to have a 'bad back'. If you sit all day, if you've injured your spinal ligaments, discs or joints, or if you have degeneration in those joints, you have probably lost some of the efficient use of your corset. If you've also always breathed poorly, if your pelvic floor is weak, if you've had a caesarean or abdominal surgery, or if you've had irritable bowel syndrome and you've always got a bloated tummy, how well you use your corset to support your spine will also be affected. And if on top of that you were born floppy and have little inherent structural support, you probably experience lots of pain. The good news is the pain doesn't have to last.

Be patient while you rebuild your corset.

How will you know if your core stability is improving?

Rebuilding your corset is a slow process, so be patient and try to become aware of small changes. Don't expect to suddenly wake up one morning, spring out of bed and be pain-free all day. Many people feel frustrated in those first few weeks that nothing seems to be happening. But if you've had back pain for a long time, perhaps 10 or 15 years, it will take at least two to three months to start to rebuild an efficient corset.

In the first six to eight weeks as your tortoise muscle fibres improve in endurance, static activities such as sitting and standing for any length of time become a little easier. Instead of getting pain after 30 minutes of sitting, it may take an hour. Don't be despondent if the pain feels the same when it does come on – the sign that you're improving is that the pain is taking longer to come on. Eventually, sitting or standing will be comfortable and you'll be able to ease any aching easily by taking a small stretch.

The next step to better stability is an increased ability to do dynamic activities like lifting and bending, not just static ones like sitting and standing. You'll start to move normally again, instead of protecting your back, 'just in case'.

The lid of the corset

Many of our body problems come from the way we breathe. That pot belly you've always had may actually be a problem with your breathing more than a problem with your stomach muscles. Poor breathing is also hard work on your neck muscles. The neck tension you can't get rid of may be caused by neck muscles overworking every time you breathe. The tension is the muscles telling you they're exhausted.

Your lungs are quite large, running from the base of your neck almost down to your waist, and are divided into lobes. The lobes are like two balloons that are always filling and emptying with air.

At the base of the lungs is the diaphragm, which forms the lid of the deep muscle corset. The diaphragm is like a piece of rubber stretched across the base of the lungs which moves up and down as you breathe in and out.

Many people have developed poor breathing habits due to a number of reasons including asthma, stress and poor posture. Inefficient breathing not only affects the lungs but may also affect how well you use your deep corset. This poor breathing can cause unnecessary tension in the neck and shoulders.

When you breathe efficiently the air automatically moves down into the lower parts of your lungs without much muscular effort. Even more importantly, as the air moves deeper into your lungs, the diaphragm drops and helps activate the stabilising muscles in your deep corset. It's a beautifully designed system as long as we breathe deeply. The poorer (or shallower) your breathing, the less the diaphragm moves and the less likely it is to work in with your lower back corset.

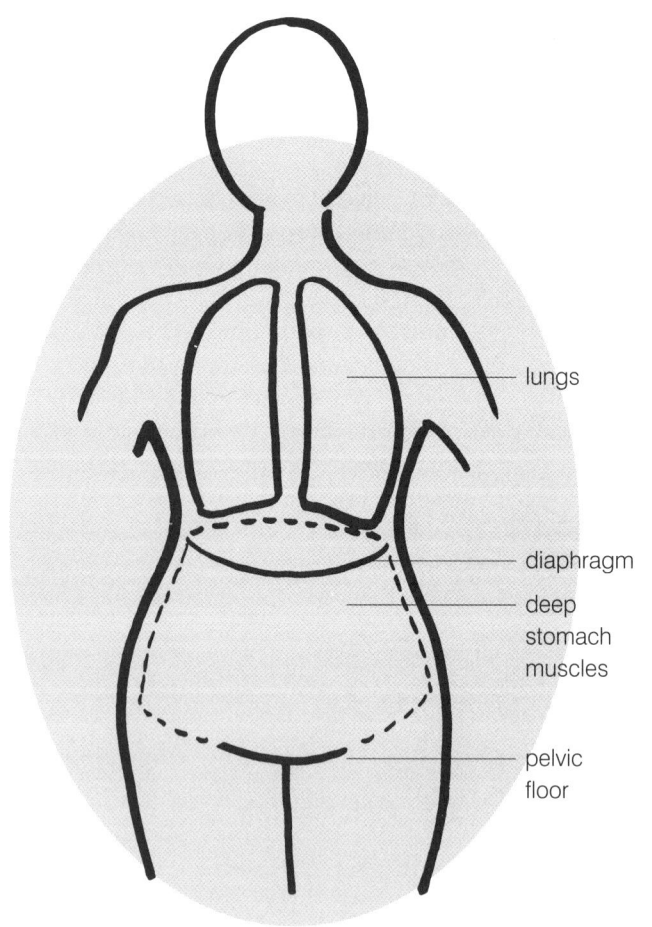

lungs

diaphragm

deep stomach muscles

pelvic floor

The first step to developing a stable core is learning to breathe well.

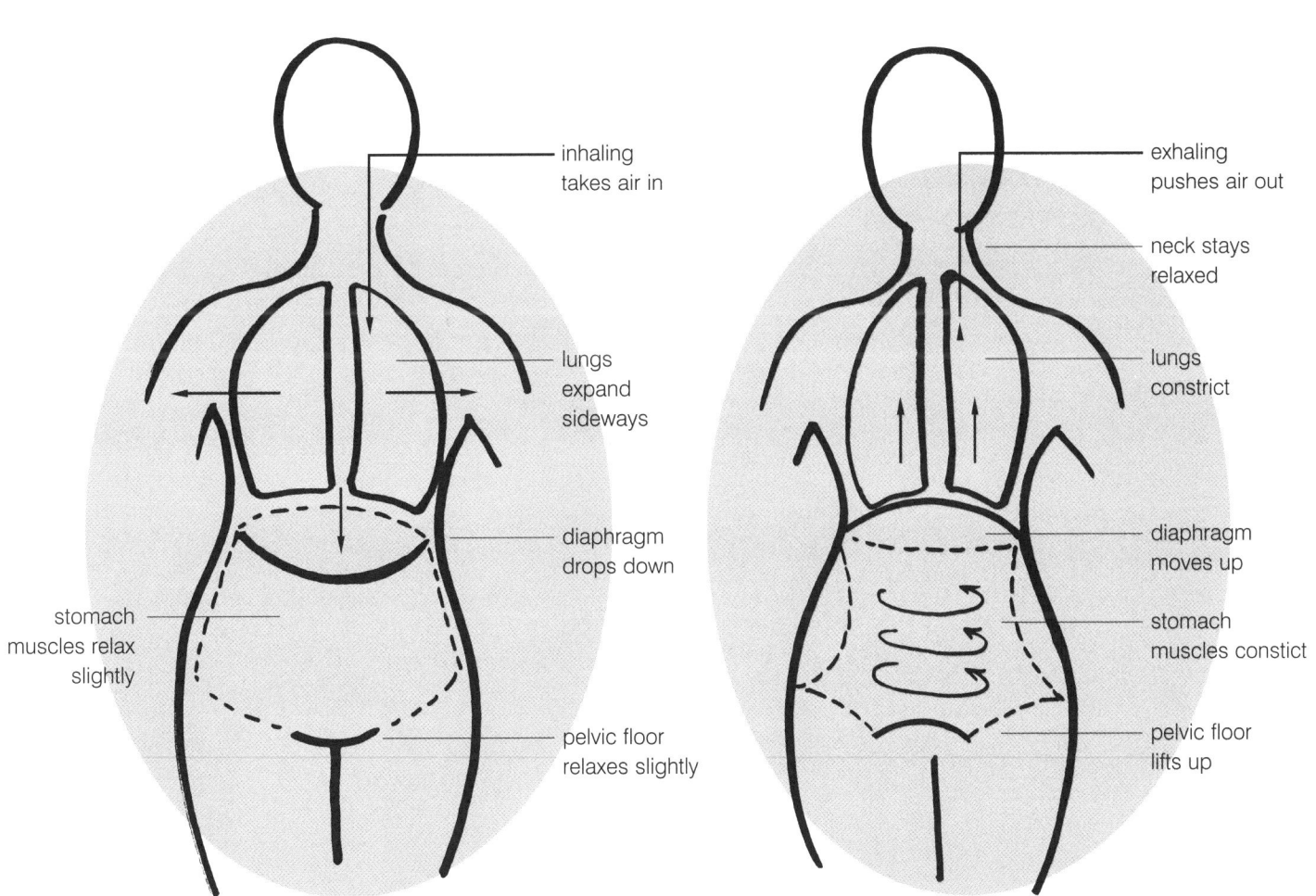

inhaling
takes air in

lungs
expand
sideways

diaphragm
drops down

stomach
muscles relax
slightly

pelvic floor
relaxes slightly

exhaling
pushes air out

neck stays
relaxed

lungs
constrict

diaphragm
moves up

stomach
muscles constict

pelvic floor
lifts up

Breathing deeper

When you breathe, the aim is to get air into your lungs as efficiently as you can. To do this you need to learn to use the whole of your lungs, not just the top parts.

How do you breathe?

Try this simple test.
● Attach your posture dots.
● Sit in front of a mirror and slump, dropping the centre dot.
● Now take a few deep breaths.
● Watch your neck and shoulders carefully. Are your shoulder dots moving up and down? Are the muscles at the front of your neck obvious and tense? If so, you're probably using only the upper parts of your lungs, your neck and your shoulder muscles when you breathe. This is hard work on those muscles.

tense neck muscles

lower lungs compressed

diaphragm squashed

deep corset off

Breathing better

Equipment
● pillow

This is a Tai Chi exercise that works beautifully to develop deeper breathing.

Starting position
● Lie on the floor with a pillow under your neck and completely relax. You may also need a pillow under your knees.

● Place your hands around the sides of your ribs, just above your waist, thumbs at the back, fingers at the front.

The movement – lying down
● Breathe in slowly and softly through your nose to a slow count of 3. Imagine the air is going all the way down to the base of your lungs and is moving your ribs sideways.

● Breathe out slowly through your nose to a count of 5. Imagine that you have a candle a few centimetres from your nose – as the breath comes out don't let the flame flicker. This visualisation will keep your breath soft and even.

● Keep breathing in and out slowly, feeling your ribs move into your hands. Don't try to fill your stomach with air. Just concentrate on moving the air into the base of your lungs and widening the ribs as the air comes down. You'll feel your ribs move in and out as you breathe in and out. Be careful that your shoulders don't lift, that your neck stays relaxed, and that you don't breathe through your mouth.

The movement – sitting
● Once you feel confident with the basic breathing exercise, sit in front of a mirror.

● Balance your bottom bones and relax your shoulders.

● Place your thumbs gently on either side of your lower ribs. Gradually practise breathing in and out without using your neck muscles.

The result
● Good control of your breathing helps good control of your lower back corset.

Learning to breath well
Use your nose! Many people's breathing problems stem from breathing through the mouth. Your nose is a filtering system housing a series of microscopic hairs designed to filter everything you breathe in that could potentially irritate your lungs.

If you're asthmatic, or prone to sinus, you'll be aware of how difficult breathing through your nose can be. Your problems with your lower back corset may be related to the problems with your breathing. You need to sort these out before you go any further. Your doctor will be able to assess whether you need medication or referral to a specialist.

The stomach wall

The stomach muscles form the walls of the lower back corset. When they work well, they also activate the deep back muscles. So strengthening your stomach wall also strengthens your back.

The stomach muscles are arranged in layers, a bit like a piece of creamy layered cake or tiramisu. Each layer plays a different role in supporting your spine as you move. Unless you understand what each does, you won't be able to develop efficient stability that protects your spine.

For years we have known that stomach exercises are important for the spine, but we didn't understand the part played by the specific layers. Now we know that the layers are made up of both tortoise and hare muscle fibres and as a result they require different strategies to improve in strength and endurance. The tortoise muscle holds you up for prolonged periods without getting tired. The hare muscle is designed to switch on for short bursts of activity like lifting, twisting or carrying.

Lots of ab crunches won't help your deep lower back corset.

Cream on top

The actual wall of muscle is only about 1 cm thick. This often surprises people as when they look down, they see an awful lot of flesh. What that is, is the 'cream' on top of the layers of muscle. The amount of 'cream' (or fat) you have depends on your diet, the genes you inherited and your hormones. Most post-menopausal women will tell you that they developed more 'cream' in their 50s with no change in their diet. While strengthening your stomach wall will not change the amount of cream you have, it will alter the diameter of your lower back corset.

The custard layer

The custard layer of muscle runs vertically from just under your breastbone to your pubic bone. It's the muscle that you activate when you do an abdominal crunch. This layer is not particularly useful for core stability. It's composed of hare muscle, so even though it can come on strongly it fatigues quickly. If it becomes overdeveloped it curls you forward – the last thing most of us need. So, doing lots of ab crunches won't help your deep lower back corset much at all.

The stomach muscles are arranged in layers like tiramisu.

The sponge layer

Have you ever laughed so much your tummy hurt? That's the sponge layer (also used for coughing and sneezing) getting tired. You have one set on each side and each set runs around to intersect with muscles in your lower back corset. If you put your hands on your stomach as if putting them in pockets, you'll feel the angle of these muscles. Because they run diagonally and around the stomach wall, they play a more important part in core stability than the muscles in the custard layer. But because they are largely hare muscle, they are mainly used for dynamic activities, particularly twisting or turning.

The deep biscuit layer

This is the deepest layer of the corset and the most important in creating a stable core. It is the only layer to wrap horizontally around the spine to work with the back muscles in stabilising your core. When it turns on, the whole circumference of your waist narrows. When it releases, the circumference widens and your stomach spreads. An efficient deep biscuit layer means a narrower, flatter stomach.

This layer contains the most tortoise muscle fibres. If you have had back pain or poor alignment for years, much of the tortoise muscle has become so weak that you rely on the hare muscle of the sponge and custard layers for support. This is very inefficient

Identifying the stomach muscle layers

This simple activity helps you find each of your stomach muscle layers. Read the whole activity first, then lie on the floor, without flattening your back. It should have a slight curve as the aim is to position your spine as if you were sitting or standing, allowing the muscles to work in a functional position.

Finding the normal curve of your spine.

● Lie on your back with your knees bent and feet flat on the floor

● Gently flatten your back as far as it will go.

● Now arch your back as far as it will go.

● Find the middle point between these two curves. If necessary, place a small folded towel under your lower back to fill in the space and allow your back to relax more.

Getting through the cream on top

● To feel these muscle layers it's best to use the third, fourth and little finger of each hand. Gently push through your cream until you notice a firmer sensation. That's the beginning of your muscle walls.

Finding the custard (top) layer

● Still lying on the floor, put one finger of one hand at the bottom of your breastbone, then slide it down about 3 cm so that it's on your diaphragm.

● Put the other hand underneath your belly button.

● Now lift your head and curl forwards in a sit-up action. You will feel the muscle bulge under your fingers.

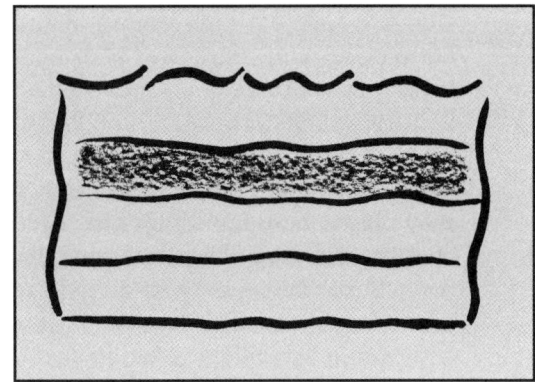

Finding the sponge (middle) layer

● Next find the front of your hip bones, which are almost in a horizontal line with your belly button.

● Put the third, fourth and fifth finger tips of each hand on these bones and then let your fingers slip into your stomach at the point it joins the bone (like a small gutter on either side). Make sure you feel through the cream until you notice the muscle wall.

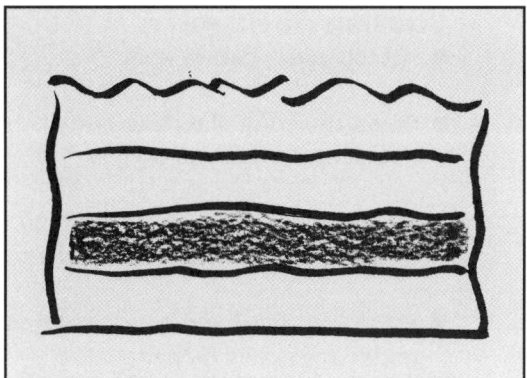

● Now cough. You'll feel the muscles under your fingers quickly bulge up into your fingers and then recede.

● Now try to harden your stomach as if someone were about to punch it. Feel the muscles bulge up quickly again. This is the sponge layer.

Finding your deep biscuit (bottom) layer

● Find your hip bones again, but this time move your fingers in about 3 cm diagonally towards your pubic bone. This is the best spot to feel the deepest layer. Don't move your fingers too close to your belly button as you will be feeling the wrong muscles.

● Gently put your finger tips through the cream a little more firmly than you have for the other layers, until you can feel the muscle wall. It can be difficult at first to recognise these deep muscles, which is why you need your fingers to feel.

● Take a slow breath in to a count of 3, then breathe out slowly to a count of 5. As you do this, slowly draw the stomach wall in as you control the breath. Don't let your spine move. You'll feel your stomach wall moving away from your fingers, much like a soufflé collapsing. You shouldn't feel the wall tense up or harden at all.

● You'll notice a soft feeling as the muscle wall draws in. If you feel a quick, bulging contraction of the wall under your fingers, you're on the top layers again.

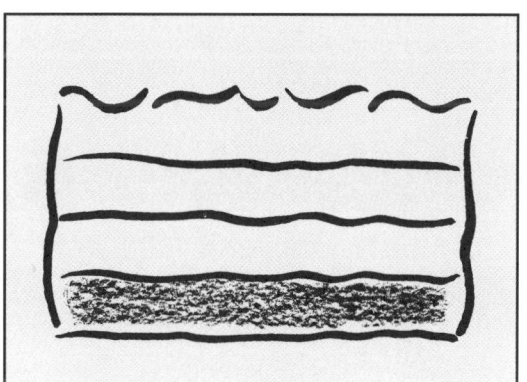

A strong deep biscuit layer
= a strong core.

Training the deep biscuit layer

Equipment
- chair
- mirror
- posture dots

You need to train the muscle of your deep biscuit layer in the position in which you will be using it – that is, sitting or standing. As you are building endurance in tortoise muscle fibres, you have to perform this action in a slow controlled way without trying too hard. Doing it quickly will activate the wrong muscles. Don't expect to feel anything dramatic, rather it's a soft drawing in of your corset. Start practising in front of a mirror and soon you will be able to do it without visual aids. By doing it repeatedly you will gradually increase your endurance and effectively support your core without conscious effort.

Starting position
- Attach your posture dots.

- Sit on the edge of a chair and balance your bottom bones.

- Place your right hand on your diaphragm, underneath your centre dot.

- Place your left hand on your stomach under your belly button.

- Now relax your neck and shoulders.

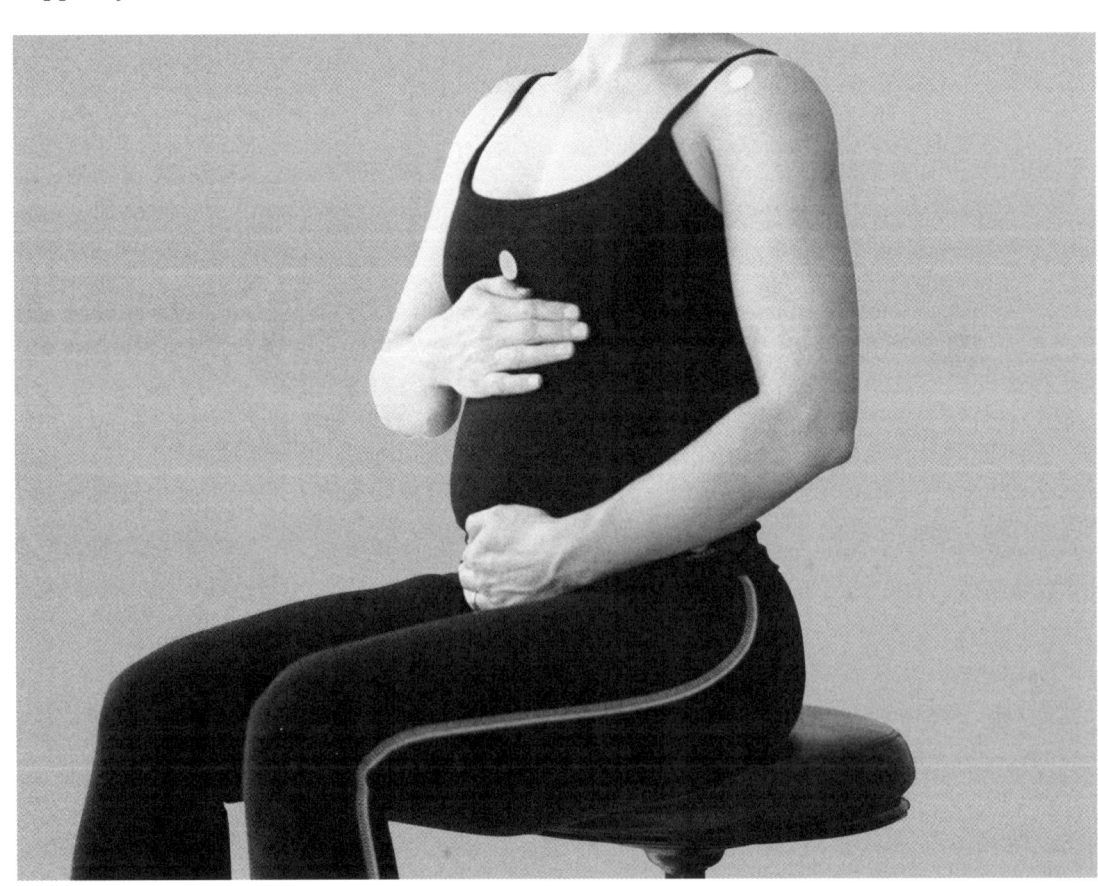

The movement

● Take a slow breath to a count of 3 keeping your shoulders relaxed. Feel your side ribs widen under your right hand. Make sure you don't over breathe and tense your diaphragm – if you fill your stomach with too much air your corset will switch off every time you breathe in.

● As you breath out slowly and softly to a count of 5, move the wall of your stomach in towards your spine. Keep your back still and don't let your centre dot drop!

● Breathe in again to a count of 3 focusing on your right hand and slightly releasing your stomach, then breathe out again to a count of 5 slowly moving your stomach in again.

Result

● Over time your stomach wall stays in, even when you're not thinking about it.

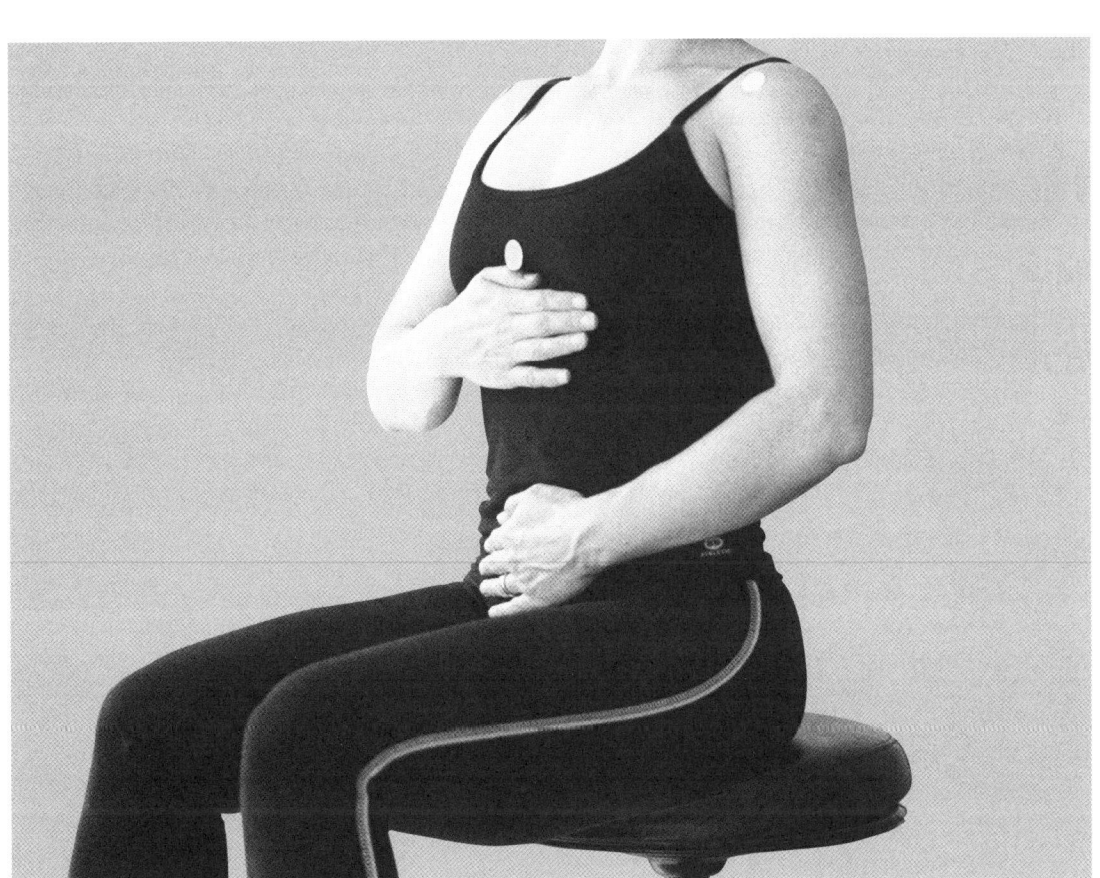

The base of the corset

The base of the corset is made up of a sling of muscles, also arranged in layers, called the **pelvic floor** muscles. Weakness in this area can destabilise the lower back corset. Fortunately, improving it is possible.

Pelvic floor muscles run from the pubic bone at the front of your pelvis through to the coccyx at the back. When the pelvic floor muscles activate, the deep biscuit layer activates as well, and vice versa. Once you learn to contract your pelvic floor muscles and keep breathing, you're on the way to having a stable corset that supports your spine.

Secret women's business
Pelvic floor weakness is extremely common in women, and not knowing what to do about it even more common.

Postnatal and post-menopausal women may notice their pelvic floors have weakened considerably. Sometimes this is because of the mechanical effects of overstretching the muscles (as happens in pregnancy) but it can also be as a result of hormonal changes which can cause softening and weakening of these muscles.

If you have backache and notice your pelvic floor is getting weaker, you probably won't associate the two. You're even less likely to associate your spreading tummy with this same problem.

Secret men's business
Most men have no idea they have pelvic floor muscles. Even though their muscles are not as susceptible to weakness, men as well as women will find using the pelvic floor is one of the most efficient ways to activate the lower back corset.

Stress incontinence or bladder weakness is more widespread in older men than many people realise. Not only will the next strategy help stabilise and build the endurance of any age of corset, it will also help men with mild stress incontinence problems.

Activate the pelvic floor to activate the lower back corset.

The secret women's business quiz

This quiz helps you work out whether your pelvic floor muscles need some work.

How many children have you had?		Score
A	none	0
B	one	1
C	two	2
D	three	3
E	more than three	4

Did they weigh more than 4 kg at birth?

A	yes	1
B	no	0
Score one extra point for each kilogram over 4		extra

Have you had any caesarean sections?

A	yes	1
B	no	0
Score one extra point for each caesarean		extra

Did you have any difficult births (e.g. long labours)?

A	yes	1
B	no	0
Score one extra point for each difficult birth		extra

Do you experience any 'leakage' when you cough or sneeze?

A	yes	1
B	no	0

How old are you?

A	under 20	0
B	21-39	1
C	40-59	2
D	60 or over	3

Have you been through menopause?

A	yes	1
B	no	0

If so, are you on Hormone Replacement Therapy (HRT)?

A	no	1
B	yes	0

Do you regularly suffer from constipation?

A	yes	1
B	no	0

If so, do you strain to pass stools?

A	most of the time	2
B	some of the time	1

Total score _____

Scoring

Add up the scores on the right side of the questions and find your total score. The closer your score is to 16, the more likely you are to have difficulty using your pelvic floor muscles with your lower back corset. If you've had a number of children and/or caesarean sections your score may even be over 16.

Score	Priority
Under 4	low
Between 5 and 10	medium
Between 11 and 16	high
Over 16	very high

Training the pelvic floor

Equipment
● kitchen bench

Try this strategy for training your pelvic floor in the standing position first. When you feel confident with the action, try it sitting on the edge of a chair with your feet apart. Alternatively, lie down on your back, feet together, and drop your knees as wide apart as you can. One of these positions will work best for you to trigger your contraction and eventually you'll be able to activate your pelvic floor in all positions.

What you are aiming for is a deep drawing in feeling as you breathe out. Initially you'll let go completely as you breathe in and then switch on completely as you breathe out. On a range of motion from zero to 10, you're moving from zero to 10. You need to work towards having your lower back corset move from about two when you breathe in to about five when you breathe out.

This strategy is useful if you have only mild to moderate degrees of weakness in your pelvic floor. But if you have significant pelvic floor weakness, either as a result of childbirth, surgery or menopause, you'll need a one-to-one assessment by your physiotherapist who can then recommend a specific program.

Like all new skills, this strategy takes time and practise to master. In the early stages, each time you breathe out consciously lift your pelvic floor. After a while this rhythm will become habit, which in turn will improve the stability of your core. You'll also know that your pelvic floor is strengthening because all the symptoms that accompany weakness, such as frequency, leaking and not being able to drink much without needing to go to the toilet, should become less of a nuisance.

Starting position
● Stand with your bottom slightly out, your feet a little apart and your toes pointing slightly inward.

● Keep your knees straight. Make sure your shoulders and neck are relaxed. Let your tummy completely relax, but don't let your back sway as you let your stomach go.

don't let the back sway

buttocks relaxed

stomach wall relaxed

toes pointing inward

The movement

- Breathe in to a slow count of 3 and then slowly breathe out to a count of 5. As you breathe out you'll gradually activate your pelvic floor.

- **For women:** imagine you have a straw coming out of your vagina with a pea on the end of the straw. As you breathe out, visualise the pea being drawn tightly onto the end of the straw. Breathe in again, but don't completely let the pea drop off the straw. Now breathe out and draw the pea in again. Slowly relax and let everything go.

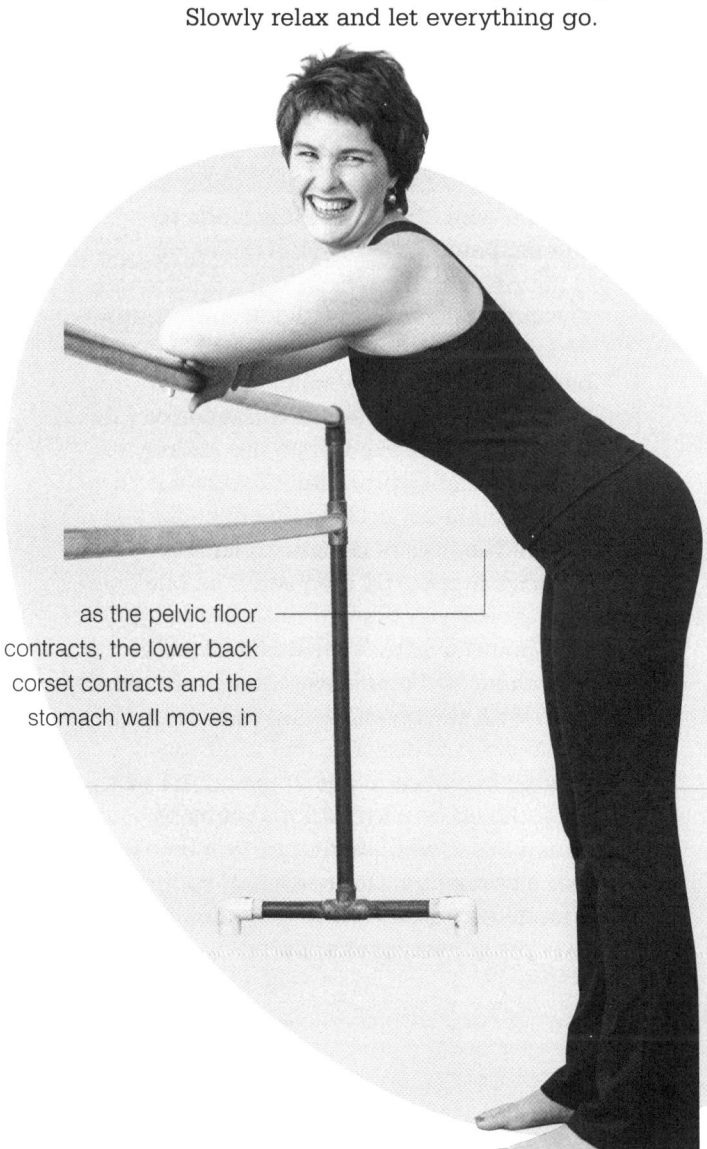

as the pelvic floor contracts, the lower back corset contracts and the stomach wall moves in

- **For men:** first, imagine you're in a lift with a person you're trying to impress when you suddenly realise that you need to pass wind. Try to stop yourself *without* squeezing your buttocks.

The result

- The wall of your stomach sucks in as you lift your pelvic floor (although you may not feel anything in your pelvic floor area).

Handy hints

- Always keep your legs apart to stop you from using your strong inner thigh muscles to 'cheat'.

- Don't let your spine move at all, in any position. Initially you're working on your static stability not your moving stability.

- Don't squeeze your buttocks.

- Breathe slowly. Start with three breaths and relax, then gradually build up to maintaining the rhythm for longer stretches.

- Don't try too hard. Soften your breath and relax more as you breath. Remember, the pelvic floor is composed of tortoise muscle fibres that work at a low grade for long periods.

- Try putting your thumb into the roof of your mouth and press it hard against your upper palette. As you do this, suck as hard as you can on your thumb. For some men and women, this sucking action triggers a strong contraction in the pelvic floor and may help give you a better feeling of where it is.

Stretching

Stretching can bring relief from muscle tension and spasm, which feels great.
Or it can be used to lengthen a stiff bit or get it moving, which feels awful but is
very good for you. Knowing what stretches you need, and what you need them for,
is the second component of supporting your core.

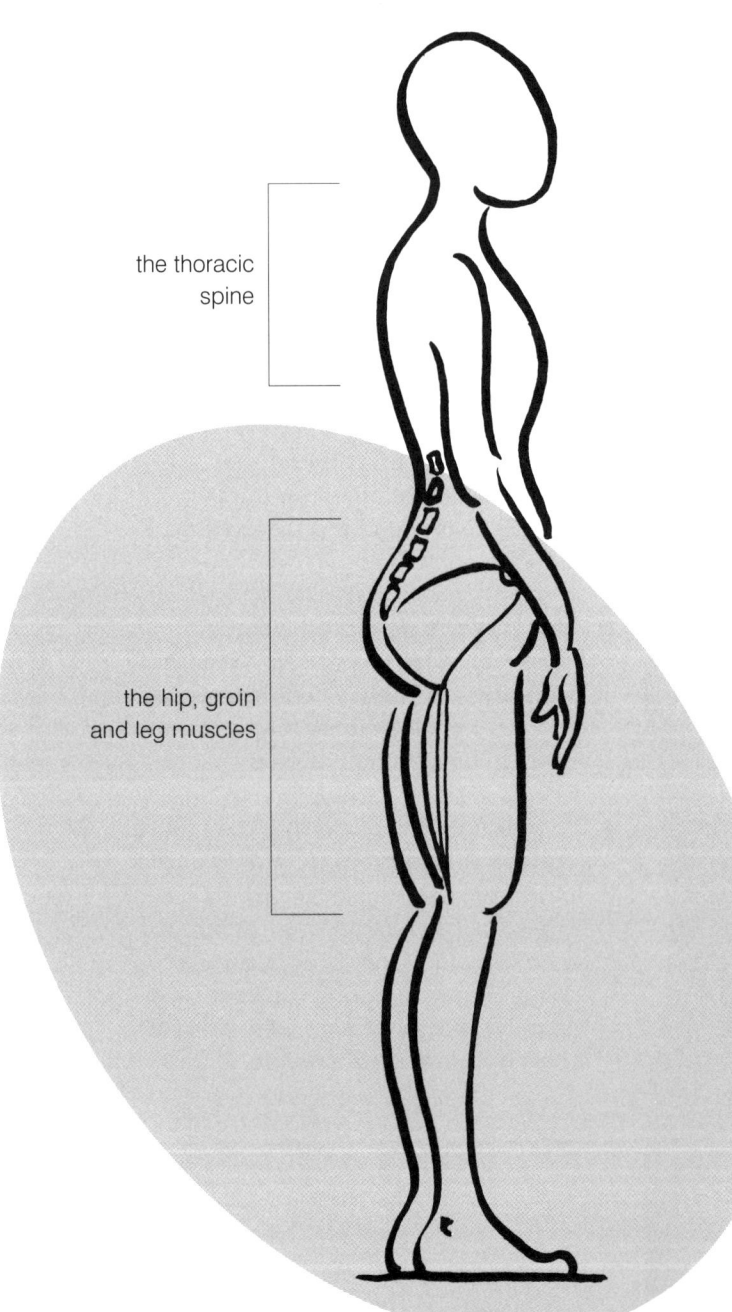

the thoracic
spine

the hip, groin
and leg muscles

Stretching for stiff bits

Moving stiff bits is particularly important
for flippies and stiffies. In a perfectly
balanced and stable spine, the loading
areas support and the moving areas (with
the help of a stable corset) move. In a
spine that is not adequately supported,
the loading areas get stiff and the moving
areas get weak and wobbly. The stiffer the
stiff bits, the more load the wobbly bits
have to take. Over time, this leads to
chronic pain.

The two main stiff bits, the thoracic spine
and the hips and pelvis, are also likely to
become stiffer if they're not well balanced.
For example, if you stand with your weight
on one leg all the time, one hip is likely to
be stiffer and tighter than the other. If you
have a slight scoliosis and your shoulders
are uneven, this is likely to make the
thoracic supporting area stiffer on one side.

Your spine is a three dimensional structure.
Stretching stiff bits is like taking a Rubik's
cube with the layers sitting slightly
twisted out of position, and then subtly
moving one section one way and the next
layer the other way until it's perfectly
square. Your whole structure will be back
into alignment with the load off your joints.
Your deep muscle corsets will then be able
to support your moving parts.

Stretching and stabilising are like a clutch and an accelerator.

Stretching for relief from tension

Stretching is also useful if you're on the floppier end of the scale. One of the reasons you develop so much muscle tension in your back is that your body is trying to compensate for a lack of core stability. If the muscles of the deep corset, especially the walls, aren't doing their job, your body compensates by producing muscle spasm in the back to try to provide support. This makes you achy and sore and stretching can provide good short term relief.

Remember, stretching your stiff bits will only be effective and long lasting if you incorporate it into your total program. Use your new freedom of movement to make the balancing strategies even easier. Once you can align yourself with less resistance from your stiff bits, it should be much easier to work on your stabilising strategies and your corset. Stretching and stabilising are like a clutch and an accelerator: as you ease one off, you may need to increase the other. Finding what works for your back takes time and some trial and error, but in the long run you'll have less pain. It's worth it!

muscle spasm can develop in the neck corset

muscle spasm can develop in the lower back corset to compensate for lack of stability

The thoracic spine

The thoracic spine extends from the base of your neck to just above your waist.
It consists of 12 vertebrae, stacked on top of one another, with 12 ribs on each side
of the torso that wrap around from front to back and protect your lungs and heart.

When you're backing out of the driveway, can you reverse the car without having to turn your whole body? If not, you've probably lost some of your thoracic rotation movement and you're compensating by using other parts of your spine, in particular your lower back joints.

Thoracic stiffness creeps up on you. Most people aren't aware they have a problem in their thoracic spine until they're quizzed about it – thoracic aching is more like a 'background noise'. Stiff areas usually don't give you the sharp jabs of pain your wobblier, unstable areas do. Instead, the thoracic area aches if you sit for any length of time. You often feel like rubbing your knuckles into your spine, or pushing your chest forward to get a 'click' to relieve the tension. The real problem starts when other, more mobile areas, such as the neck and lower back, start to compensate for thoracic stiffness.

When you turn or bend, there should be movement in many areas of the spine. When you turn your head, for example, the vertebrae in your neck rotate to allow you to move. However, to fully turn your head, the vertebrae in your thoracic spine should also move, all the way to your mid shoulder blades. If the thoracic area is stiff, the neck area (a wobbly bit) compensates by increasing the amount of movement in its joints. After a while the neck can become stressed and you feel pain.

When you try to sit up straight you might also be using a compensatory movement. If your thoracic spine is stiff, you'll often compensate by overarching in the lower back in an effort to straighten up. After a while this is too much work for the lower back joints and they start to ache. So what do you do? Slump! Loosening up the thoracic area allows the load to be distributed more evenly along your whole spine.

Thoracic stiffness creeps up on you.

Think of 22 players in a team. Imagine that 12 of them hardly do any work. Over a period of time, the remaining 10, who do most of the work, gradually break down as they continue to compensate for the lazy ones. The ones doing all the work hurt the most – if you keep resuscitating the hard workers, without dealing with the lazy ones, you'll never solve the cause of the problem.

This is the way most of us approach treating our back. We get short term treatment when the wobbly weak bits have had enough, but never really look at why they keep breaking down.

For long-term relief, make the lazy bits work harder.

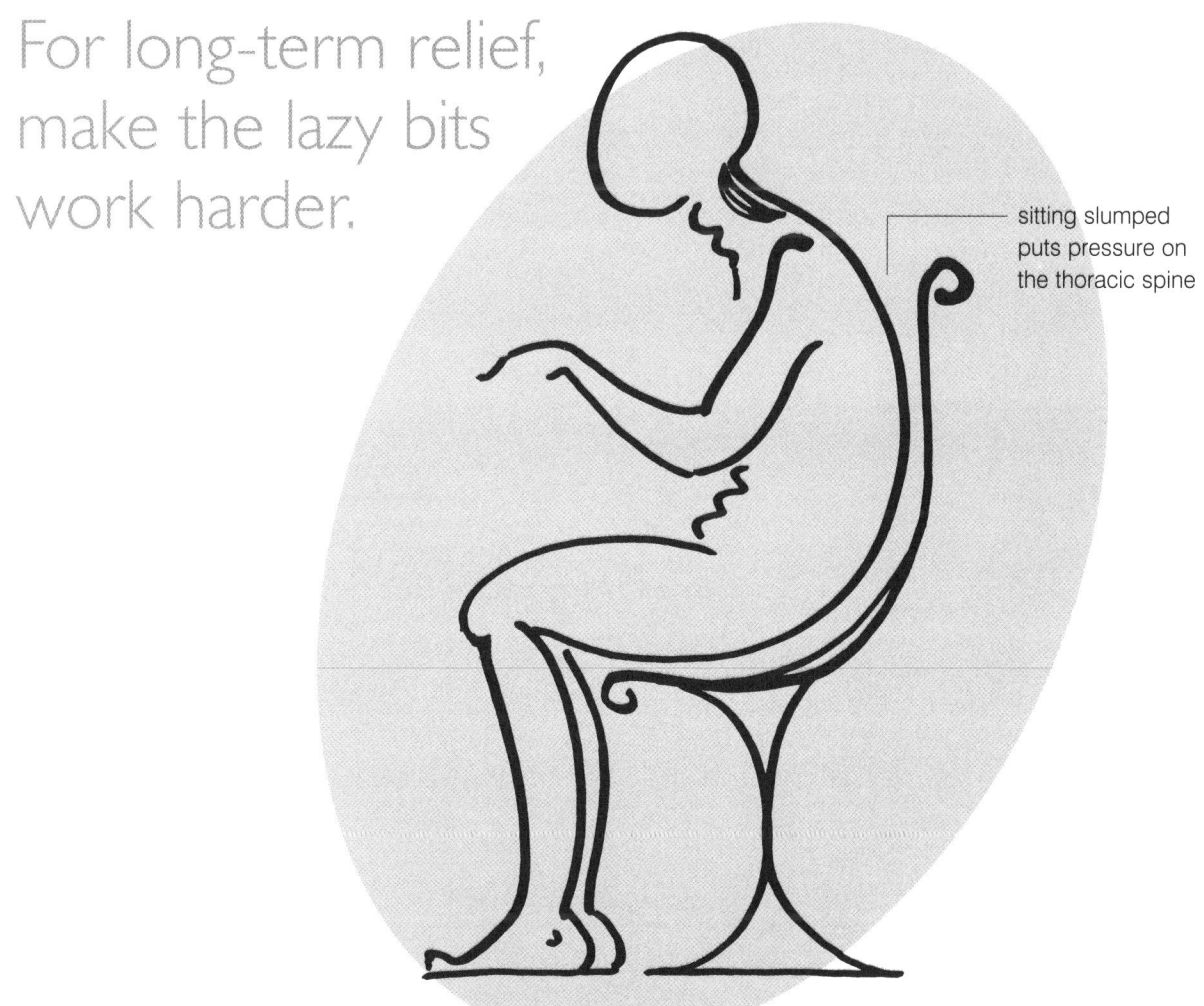

sitting slumped puts pressure on the thoracic spine

Table stretch

Equipment
● balcony rail or fence rail, about 1.1 m high

The table stretch feels good and quickly relieves pain, not only in the thoracic but also the lower back.

Starting position
● Place your hands on the balcony rail. If you can't find anything to stretch from, put your whole hand on a kitchen bench top and gently stretch back without letting your hands slide. Although not as effective as using something horizontal to pull on, sometimes a pole will work.

● Slowly walk back until you feel your armpits stretch and the sides of your waist extend.

● Keep your feet together.

Good for
Relieving general aches and pains, and stiffness after every hour of sitting.

How often
After prolonged sitting and standing as required.

back too arched

legs too straight

too much stress on shoulders

back too sway

a vertical bar can also be effective

The movement

● Move your bottom as far away from your hands as you can without letting your back arch. Imagine your spine is like a table on which you could put a plate without it falling off. If your thoracic spine is very stiff the stretch could initially look more like the Sydney Harbour Bridge.

● Now gently unlock your knees a little and hold for 20 seconds.

● Relax. You'll feel a lovely stretch underneath your armpits. The floppier you are, the more you'll feel the stretch lengthening and releasing your whole spine.

The result

● Your back muscles are relaxed and you're able to bend forward more easily.

back is lengthened

legs are relaxed

weight in the heels

Seated chair twist

Equipment
- chair
- posture dots
- mirror

The chair twist is good for helping that dull ache between your shoulder blades and into your neck when you have to sit for a long time.

Starting position
- Attach your posture dots.

- Position chair sideways to a mirror.

- Sit forward on the edge of a chair, knees together.

- Place your left hand across your right knee with your palm away from you.

- Placing your right hand into the inside of the back of the chair, push through the palm.

- Bend your right elbow until your right shoulder relaxes and the right posture dot becomes even with the left posture dot.

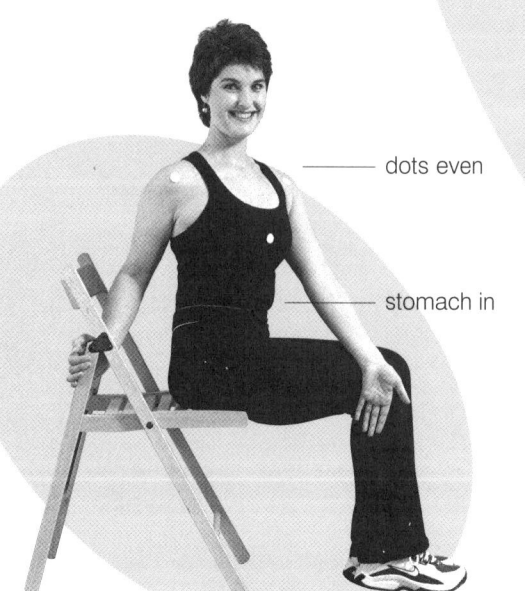

——— dots even

——— stomach in

The movement
● Slowly breathe in and as you breathe out gently turn yourself to the right. Relax the shoulder rather than lifting it and keep your neck long and chin tucked in. Be careful not to let your neck turn more than your chest as this can give you neck pain and a headache.

Good for
Aching mid-back neck tension after long periods of sitting as required.

How often
After every hour of sitting.

● Hold for 5 seconds.

● Breathe in again and push a little further as you breathe out.

● Hold for 5 seconds.

● Breathe in again and push a little further as you breathe out again.

● Hold for 10 seconds and relax.

● Repeat on other side.

The result
● A good stretch between your shoulder blades and sometimes your chest.

triangle collapsed

stomach switched off

The hip, groin and leg muscles

Stretching tight hips, groin and leg muscles is often one of the most neglected and yet most important parts of fixing chronic back pain for good.

The hip, groin and leg muscles are attached to either your spine or your pelvis (or sometimes both) so they affect the way the spine is aligned. As well as compensating for stiffness in the thoracic spine, the lower back also often compensates for tightness in the hip, groin and leg area. If these muscles are very tight they'll pull the spine into either a too swayed or too slumped position.

This tightness may be because of the way you were born (as is the case with stiffies) or it could be as a result of years of bad posture. The more we sit, the tighter these muscles become. They are also extremely tight in growing children and teenagers, when they fight to keep pace with the elongating bones underneath. Stretching these muscles can be the simplest way to improve a child's posture.

The psoas muscles

The strong psoas muscles lead from the either side of your groin to each leg. Starting in your back, they cross through the inside of your stomach and finish in the groin. They are often the first muscles to be implicated in back pain, largely because they grow short from long periods of sitting.

When the psoas muscles are very tight they increase a sway back by pulling on the lumbar vertebrae from the front. If you have a marked sway back, stretching these muscles not only gives relief to your back pain, but also often allows for easier activation of the lower stomach muscles because the spine is in a more relaxed position.

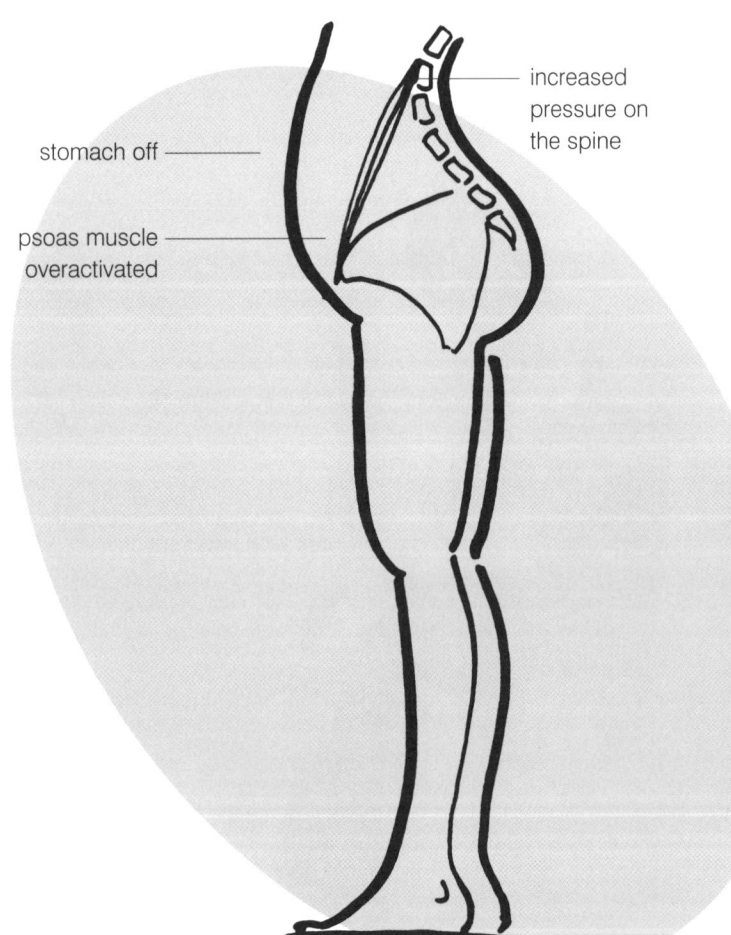

increased
pressure on
the spine

stomach off

psoas muscle
overactivated

The deep buttock muscles

The buttock muscles also have layers. The muscle we most think about when we consider our buttocks is generally the one we can see, the gluteus maximus. There are several more layers of muscles in our buttocks, the deepest of which can cause problems by going into spasm. The sciatic nerve is close to this area as it passes through the buttocks to the leg. As a result,

deep buttock spasm can cause considerable irritation to the nerve, sometimes resulting in dull leg pain. Although often mistaken for 'sciatica', that leg pain could literally be just a pain in the butt.

The deep buttock muscles are often engaged to compensate for lack of stability in the lower back. They can also be affected by standing on one leg more than the other. You'll probably find that the leg you usually stand on has the more irritable deep buttock muscle. For flippies with considerable muscle imbalance, stretching this area is particularly good for relieving dull aches in the lower back and legs.

The hamstring and calf muscles

The hamstrings are a group of muscles running from your bottom bones to the back of your knee. If they're tight they also affect the alignment of the spine through their attachment to the pelvis.

The calf muscles attach just above the knee and run down to the Achilles tendon at the back of the ankle. Generally, if your hamstrings are tight, your calves will be too.

Flippies and stiffies are usually tightest in these muscles. A sedentary job will tighten them, as will regularly wearing high heels and frequent bouts of sciatica over many years. Whatever the reason, gently stretching these muscles is excellent for relieving the load on your lower back.

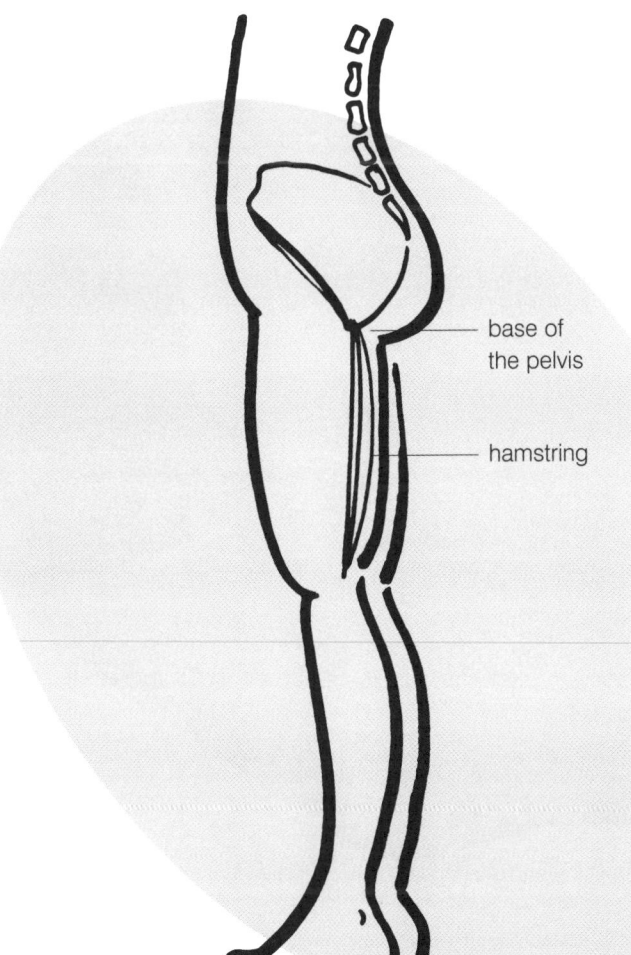

base of
the pelvis

hamstring

Psoas stretch

Equipment
● bar or bench, approximately hip height

If you're a floppy or flippy with a sway back, this exercise will give you enormous relief.

Starting position
● Hold onto the bar or bench.

● Lunge your right leg back as far as you can go and rest the knee on the floor.

● Place your hands on either side of the left foot and keep your body weight over the left leg.

Good for
Relieving aching back pain.
Lengthening your stride.

How often
Relief after a long walk .
After a prolonged period of sitting.

The movement
● Gently extend your right heel until the knee comes off the ground and no more than 5 cm (otherwise you'll lose the impact of the stretch)

● Hold for 10 seconds (your leg may shake).

The result
● A deep stretch in your right groin and at the front of your right hip or thigh.

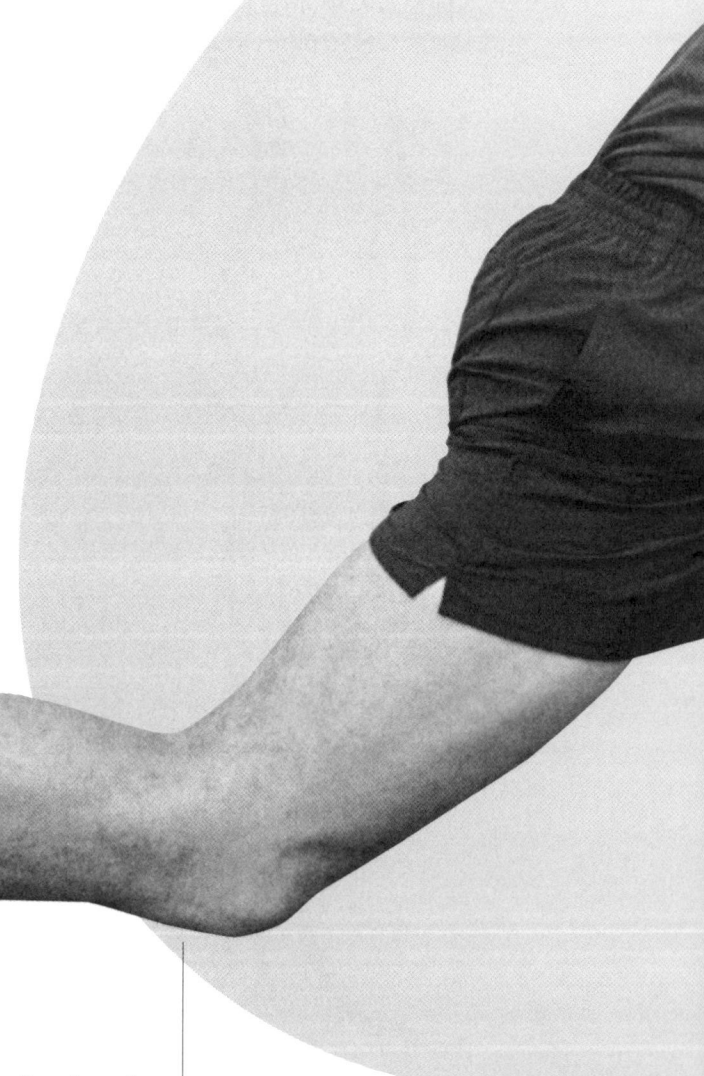

push your ankle back

knee 5cm from floor

stretch after sitting

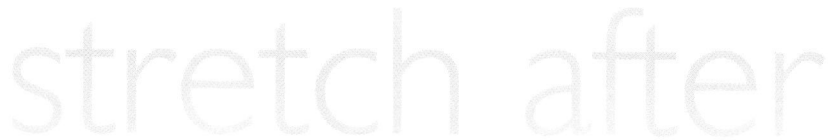

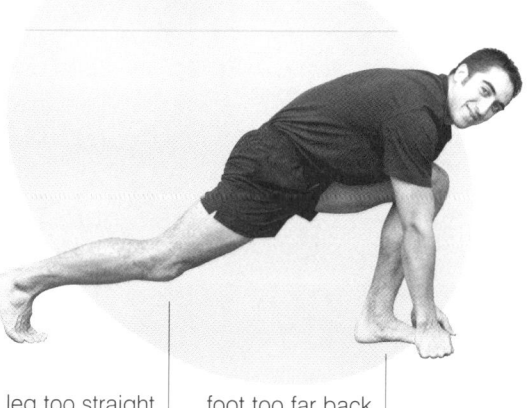

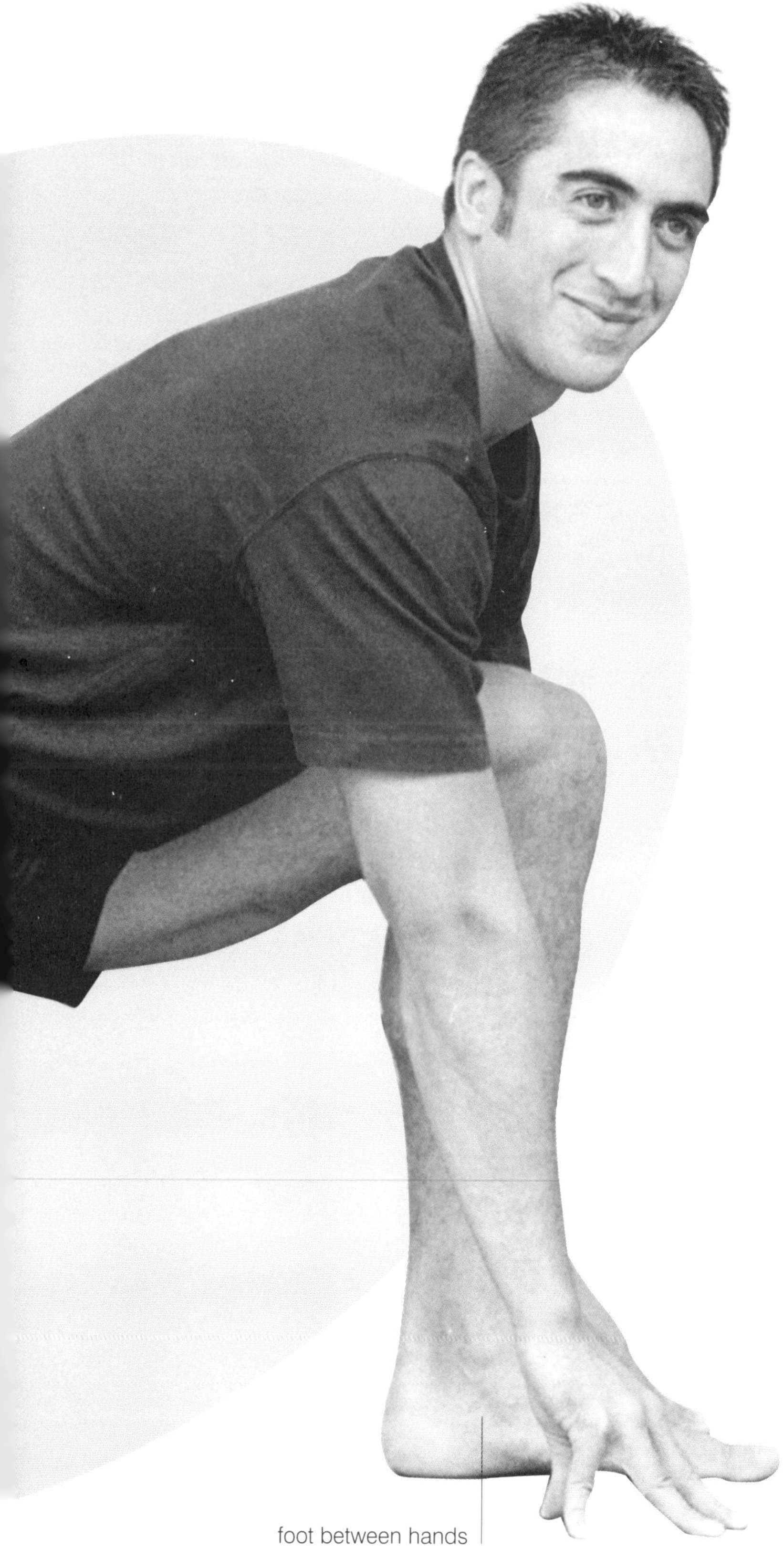
foot between hands

leg too straight
foot too far back

Buttock stretch

Equipment
- chair
- posture dots

Often the easiest way to know if you have a spasm and tightness in your buttock muscles is to gently poke your finger into one of the cheeks. If you feel a nasty little knot there, you probably need to stretch your buttocks to relieve the tension in the muscles, the nerve and, in turn, the lower back.

This is the simplest stretch. It can be done anywhere and only takes a few seconds. If you have dull back or buttock pain on one side more than the other, this stretch will help.

Starting position
- Attach your posture dots.

- Sit on the edge of a chair.

- Cross your right ankle over your left knee.

- Sit up straight.

Good for
Relieving aching buttock and back pain after lots of sitting.

How often
As needed for relief. Stiffies and flippies will probably need to do it daily to improve their movement.

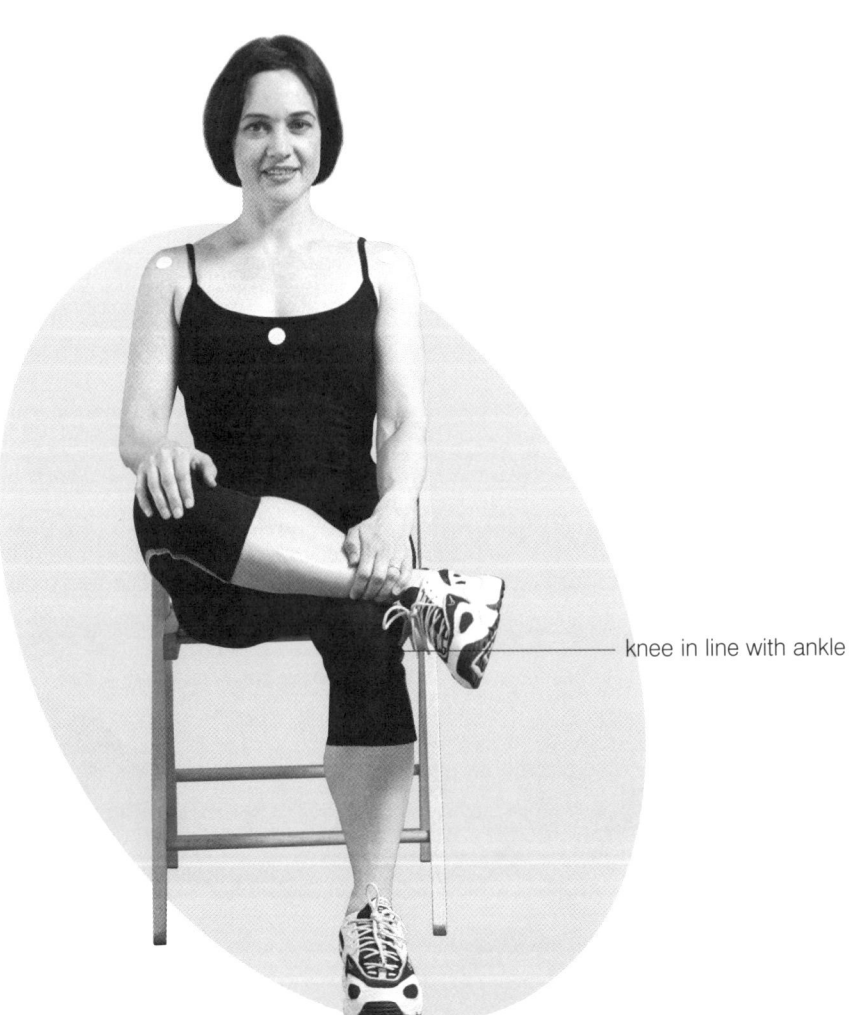

knee in line with ankle

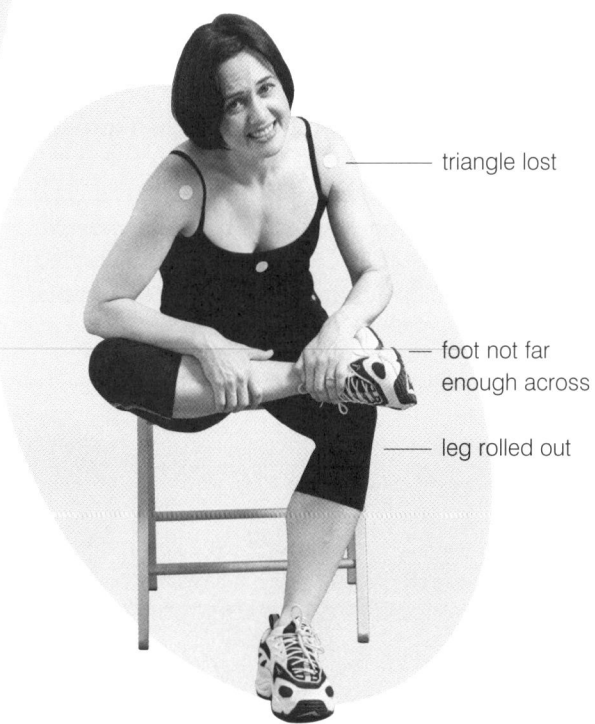

The movement

- Lift your centre posture dot.

- Keep it up as you gently move forward. Always stretch gently so that you feel good in a slightly uncomfortable way – never push to pain, particularly a sharp pain.

- When you will feel a strong stretch feeling in your hip and buttock, stop.

- Gently put your right elbow into the inside of the right knee then press down a little to increase the stretch.

- Hold for 30 seconds, then repeat on the other side. You may notice a big difference between the amount you can move on one side compared to the other. If so, do twice as many stretches on the tight side.

The result

- Relief from dull, aching buttock and lower back pain.

99

triangle lost

foot not far enough across

leg rolled out

Hamstring stretch

Equipment
● the floor

Good for
Improving your ability to sit, stand and walk.

How often
About 3 times a week if you are on the stiffer side.

Hamstring stretching can be stressful on your back if it's not done correctly. One of the worst ways is the classic 'leg up on a fence' position as this can place enormous stress on the sciatic nerve. Make sure you do this stretch exactly as shown so that the lower back is completely relaxed, and the hamstrings and calves can be gently stretched without risk of aggravating your lower back.

Done gently, this is a simple and safe stretch. Only do it if you have no acute back pain, and have not had an acute episode in the previous six months.
If you feel any pins and needles or tingling in your foot, do not continue to stretch as this may mean your sciatic nerve is still irritated. Always consult your physician if you experience acute pain.

You may be one of the many people who has always had tight hamstrings.
No matter how much you try to stretch them, they never seem to improve. It's important to not only stretch the hamstring but also the buttock and calves, as tightness in one will always result in the other trying to compensate. Sometimes the reason a muscle won't let go is because it is still trying to compensate for other structures.

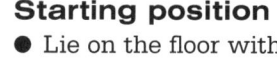
Starting position

● Lie on the floor with your right leg bent at the knee, to form a right angle to the floor, and your left leg straight. This position allows you to gently stretch your hamstring muscle without straining your back.

● Interlock your fingers behind your right thigh.

The movement

● Gently extend your lower right leg as if you're trying to straighten your leg, but don't let the thigh change position. Be careful never to overstretch. Try to pull your toes a little. You should only feel a strong stretch, not pain or pins and needles. If you do, let the foot position go.

● Feel the stretch in the back of your leg. Hold for 5 seconds.

● Repeat slowly 10 times.

The result

● The muscles at the back of your thigh are stretched.

lower leg only moves

thigh at 90°

toes to ceiling

knee locked

Calf stretch

Equipment
● kitchen bench, bar or railing, about hip height

This stretch combines several different calf stretches and allows you to stabilise your back as you stretch.

Starting position
● Gently position yourself as illustrated.

● Keep your back foot facing directly forward and do not let the toes rotate out.

● Keep your back heel locked on the ground and keep your back thigh locked. There should be almost no pressure on the front foot.

The movement
● With your arms extended in front, push with the heel of your hands into the bar. Don't let your fingers push, your back arch or your hips rotate. It's also important that you keep your back straight when you do this stretch.

● Hold for at least 30 seconds.

● Repeat on the opposite side.

The result
● Your calf stretches.

Good for
Improving bending, carrying and walking.

How often
A few times daily if you are on the stiffer side.

chest too high

back swayed

hips uneven

feet turned out

fingers in good position

back straight

hips even

knee locked

feet in line

part three

Making you stronger

Strong limbs contribute significantly to dynamic stability. To build your stability, you need to focus on two key muscle groups: your buttocks and legs and your shoulder blades and arms. Developing dynamic stability means using your corset with 'the works' – your hydraulic leg and buttock system (taking the load off your low back) coupled with your shoulder blades and arms (taking the load off your neck).

The importance of strength

You'll know the time has come to build dynamic stability and strength because your pain will be decreasing, while your tolerance to static activities such as sitting and standing will be increasing.

Strength has two aspects: power and endurance. Unless you address both aspects you'll never have a dynamically strong, low-risk back. Power is your capacity to do a 'loaded' activity for a short period of time. For example, you need power in your legs to be able to squat with bent knees and a straight spine, and then lift something. Endurance is the ability of the leg muscles to repeat a given action several times without losing your form.

Some people try to build their strength to a point far beyond the capacity of their core foundation. As a result, they recruit the wrong muscles to try to achieve a movement. Sometimes it's better to do an easier movement with good form than to try something that's too difficult. For example, fitballs are good for strengthening a number of different muscles and for challenging your dynamic stability. But before you try to strengthen your body on the fitball's wobbly surface, you need to be able to maintain your core stability on a chair or a surface that doesn't move. If you're still tending to compensate for weakness by using the wrong muscles, the fitball will make you compensate more rather than less. Instead of getting stronger, you're likely to end up with more pain.

On the other hand, some people become so afraid of hurting their back they turn around by moving only their eyeballs, ankles and feet. If you try to 'protect' your back in this way you'll have no core stability. As you learn to activate your deep corset to support your back when your turn or bend, you'll no longer look like a penguin and you'll move normally. Only then should you strengthen your outer muscles, otherwise you'll end up with more pain.

If you can't turn on your corset and sustain normal breathing, or if you still feel vulnerable when you move and bend, continue to practice the strategies in Part 2. If you don't think you're ready or able to strengthen, also consider having your local physiotherapist or physician check how you're progressing.

One final warning: The less you have to compensate for old limb injuries (such as knee and shoulder problems), the easier it will be to develop your body's dynamic stability. So, before you start the strengthening strategies, make sure you have any problems assessed. Consult a specialist physician recommended by your local doctor. Alternatively, a primary contact practitioner such as a physiotherapist or chiropractor may be helpful in settling your joint problems.

Strengthening your legs

Your legs act as your body's hydraulic system and have an important part to play in maintaining the health of your spine. Strong lower limbs provide support for the corset when you bend and twist and make your system more stable.

Most people, particularly women, know they should lift with bent knees and straight backs, but because their legs aren't strong enough to get them down and up again in the same movement they don't. In Asia there appears to be a lower incidence of back pain than in Western countries. One reason for this is that people frequently use the squatting position, giving them stronger and more flexible hydraulic leg systems.

If you have problems with your hips, knees and ankles, the way you lift and bend usually changes over time, placing a greater load on your back. You may not associate the problems in your legs with the pain in your back, but this is often the crucial missing link. If you've had a knee problem for a long while that prevents you from squatting on that side, you have probably always slightly compensated by increasing the movement in your spine to allow you to bend and lift. Over time this is likely to cause new problems in your spine because it's doing a job it wasn't designed to do. The original problem was the knee, but the result was back pain. So, to fix your back you need to improve your knee.

You can strengthen your buttocks and legs with simple everyday strategies and by becoming more aware of bad habits. You can then develop new habits that encourage the use of the right muscles more often. A simple strategy such as re-arranging the kitchen cupboards can make a significant difference. If you move frequently used items to the bottom cupboards instead of having them high up, you'll have to squat every time you get something. This will gradually strengthen your legs.

Strengthening your shoulder blades and arms

The muscles between your shoulder blades play a significant role in supporting your mid-back when you sit and stand for long periods. If these muscles are strong and efficient you'll be able to keep your chest raised and forward. If they are weak, your shoulders will drop and your chest slump. Once you've learnt to lift your posture dots, you can progress to building strength in the muscles that hold your shoulder blades down and back.

Similarly, the weaker your arms, the more you'll use your neck to compensate. If you spend a lot of time doing small movements with your hands, such as working at a keyboard, the larger arm muscles will get weaker and weaker. As the shoulders get rounder and the shoulder blade muscles let go, much of the load is transferred to the upper neck muscles and you end up with constant tension and stress across the base of your neck and shoulders. As you work on the power and endurance in your arm muscles, both your mid back and your neck will improve.

Strengthening your buttocks

Equipment
- posture dots

Your buttocks muscles play two key roles: they take the load off your spine (endurance) and propel you when you walk (power). Your deep buttock muscles sometimes become tight and exhausted because the big muscles on top, the gluteus maximii, are not doing their job adequately. To take the load off your spine you need to develop buttocks of steel. If you have weak buttock muscles, especially common in women, it may mean you can only turn on your buttocks with other, stronger muscles, particularly the hamstrings. If you find that, despite a steady commitment to walking or running, your buttock muscles never seem to get any firmer, your hamstrings are probably compensating for them. Your legs are firm but your buttocks stay soft.

How well can you use your buttocks?

Starting position
- Attach your posture dots.

- Stand with your feet shoulder width apart and parallel, and your knees locked.

- Put your hands on your buttocks then feel with your fingers until you find two hard bones deep in your buttocks, at the very base where they join your legs.

The movement
- Contract your buttocks as hard as you can keeping your legs straight.

- Now unlock your knees so that your legs are slightly bent. Don't allow your knees to straighten.

- Leave your hands on your buttocks and try to contract them without letting your posture dots drop.

- For many people, this is very difficult. When the knees are bent it is impossible to cheat and use the hamstring muscles at the back of your thighs.

What this test tells you
- If you found this test difficult, you need to learn to strengthen your buttocks without other muscles compensating. The bottom clenching strategy will help you do this.

Bottom clenching

Equipment
- credit card or Physiocise 'bottom clencher' (pictured)
- posture dots

Strong buttocks mean you'll be able to use them when your deep corset is getting fatigued. For example, when you've been standing for hours and your back is aching, you can engage your buttock muscles to give you another half hour of standing without undue aching. The bottom clenching exercise will help you do this by building endurance and tone.

Starting position
- Attach your posture dots.

- Stand with your feet shoulder width apart and parallel.

- Unlock your knees.

- Lift your dots.

The movement
- Hold your credit card, or bottom clencher, in your right hand with your index finger on one of the shorter sides of the card.

- Relax your buttocks then gently place the credit card between your cheeks.

- Keeping your knees soft and unlocked, hold the card there for 60 seconds, then let go. Be careful to keep your centre dot lifted at all times.

The result
- Within weeks your buttocks feel more like firm melons than mousse.

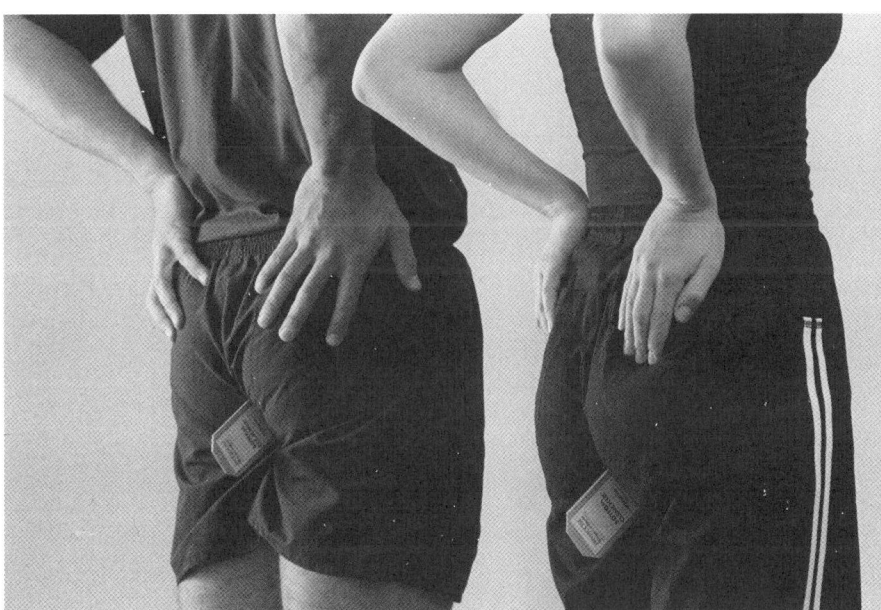

A firm bottom helps support a stable spine.

Bottom walking

Using your bottom while walking is the power-building stage of strengthening your buttocks. Your buttocks are like small retro rockets – they'll give you a burst of power when you need to walk up a hill or walk more quickly.

The key to effective bottom walking is to turn one buttock off while the other is turning on. If you always leave them on together you'll look as though you have something permanently wedged between them!

Starting position

● Stand as if you're about to take a step, with your left leg forward and your right leg back.

● Your left heel is about to hit the ground firmly. Keep the right leg relaxed.

● Put your hand on your right buttock.

bottom relaxed —————

Stronger buttocks means stronger walking.

————— lead with the heel

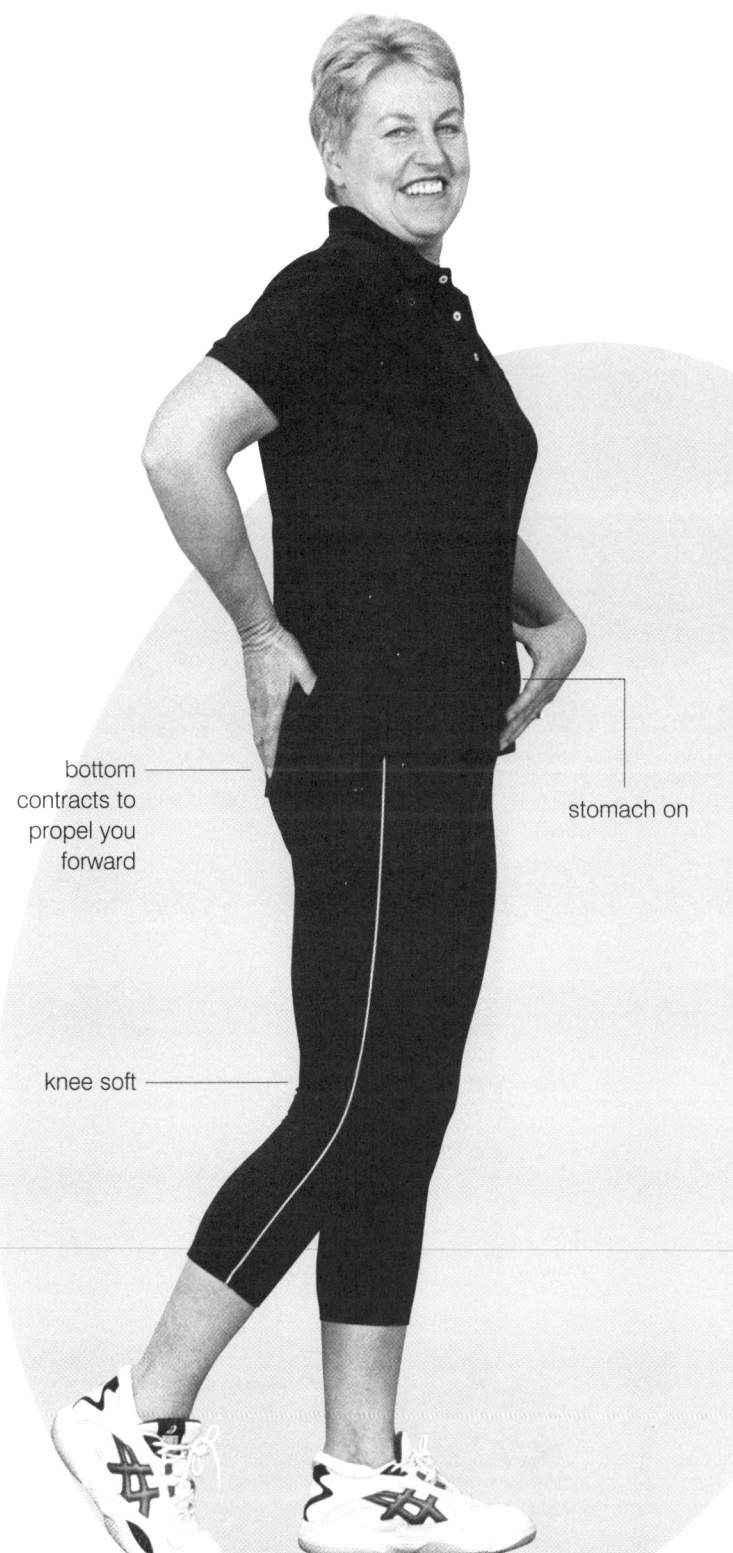

bottom contracts to propel you forward

stomach on

knee soft

The movement
● Transfer your weight forward onto the left leg by contracting the right buttock.

● Imagine the right buttock is pushing your weight forward onto the left foot. Keep your knees soft and unlocked.

● Move your weight back onto the right leg and let the right buttock relax.

● Repeat several times, turning the buttock on to go forward and off to go back.

● Now try it with the other leg.

The result
● Your weight rocks forward and back.

Try this
● Walk fairly quickly, pushing yourself forward using the buttock of the back leg. Focus on alternate buttocks pushing you forward, being careful not to stiffen your knees. Make sure your head is steady and that you're not swaying from side to side.

● Lead with your heel when you walk as this helps trigger your bottom muscles. You could also try pushing a stroller or a shopping trolley up a hill. This will help you feel your retro rockets in action.

● This leads to more efficient walking with a stable spine, longer stride, less movement through your trunk and less fatigue.

Legs-for-stairs

Equipment
- posture dots
- stairs
- mirror

To activate your buttocks and thighs, do this exercise every time you go up a step or a flight of stairs. Regular practice builds the tone in your thighs and calves, taking the load off your knee and hip joints. Initially use a mirror so you can see how you go up and down stairs.

Starting position
- Attach a posture dot in the centre of each knee cap and on each hip at the front of the boniest point of your pelvis

- Place your toe on the first stair.

Glide up and down stairs.

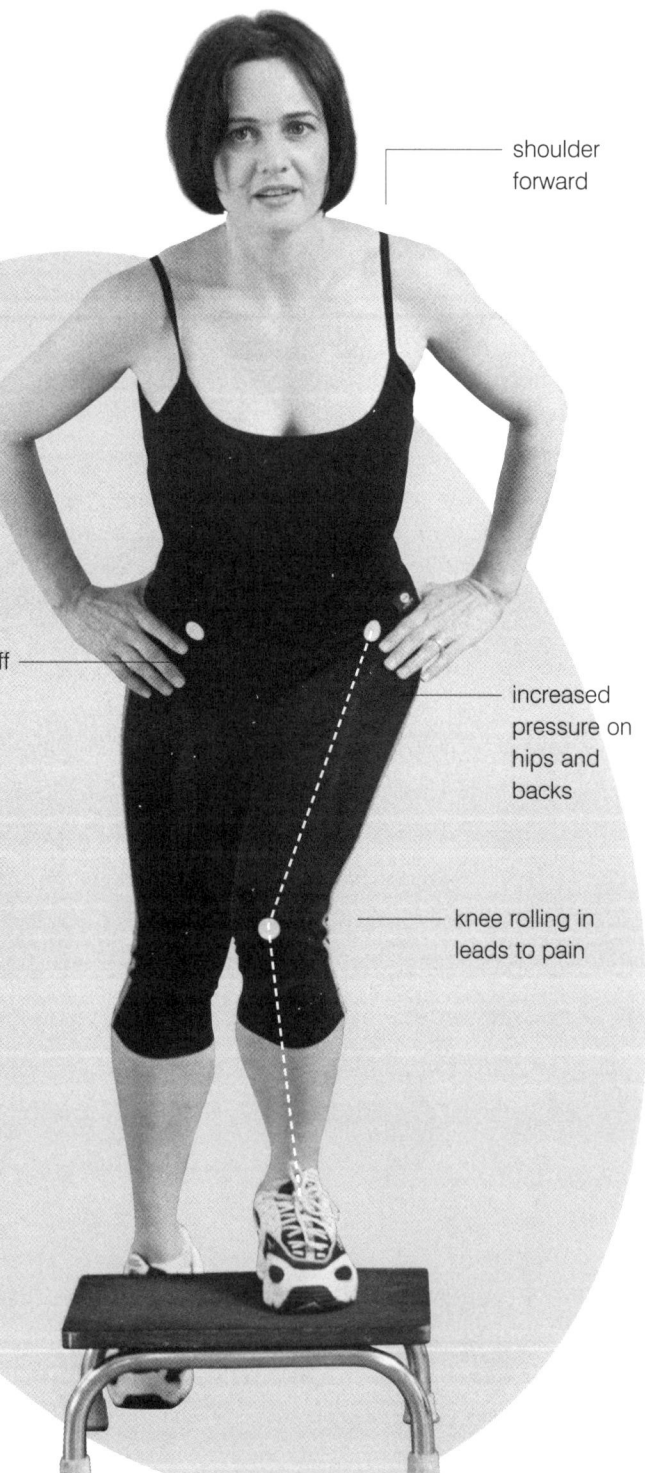

shoulder forward

tummy off

increased pressure on hips and backs

knee rolling in leads to pain

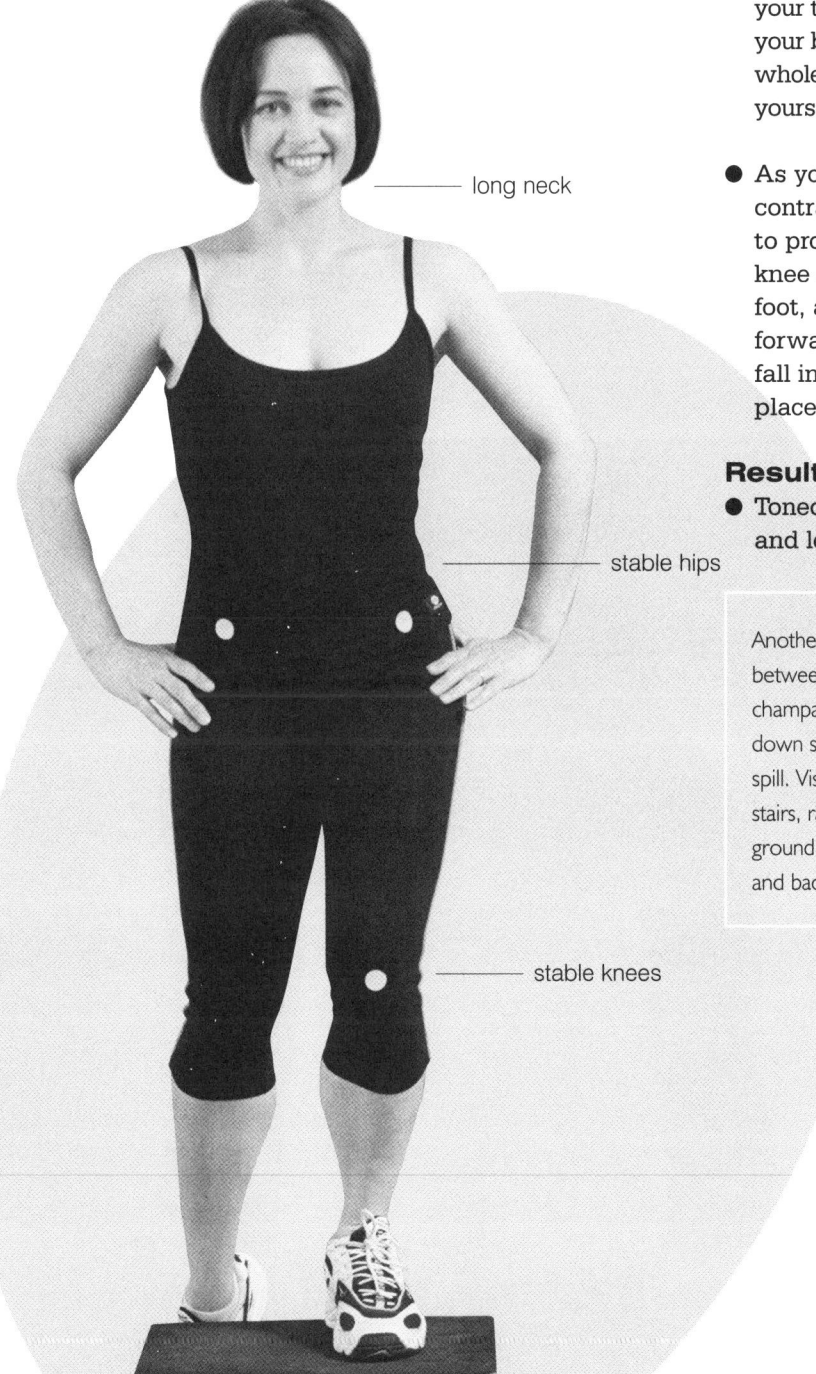

long neck

stable hips

stable knees

The movement

- Step on the edge of each stair with your toe. This makes it easier to use your buttock instead of putting your whole foot on the stair and dragging yourself up.

- As you move your weight forward contract the buttock of your back leg to propel you up the stair. Keep the knee dot over your second toe of your foot, and keep your weight coming forward not back. If you let your knee fall in or your hip dots drop, you'll place too much stress on your knees.

Result

- Toned buttocks, stronger thighs and less stress on your knees.

Another strategy to try is to imagine a tray between your two hip dots with a full glass of champagne sitting on it. Whenever you go up or down stairs, walk or stand, don't let the glass tip or spill. Visualise gliding your pelvis up or down the stairs, rather than lurching. Take any changes in the ground through your legs, not through your hips and back.

Shoulder blades and arms

Once you have a stable, mobile base with good hydraulics, you can easily strengthen your shoulder blade and arm muscles by simply using three key words: back and down. So, to release tension of hunched up and forward shoulders think about rolling them not only back but down.

Everyday activities will strengthen your arms and shoulders. Even though you may not feel anything, every time you use the right muscles in the right way, you're making them stronger.

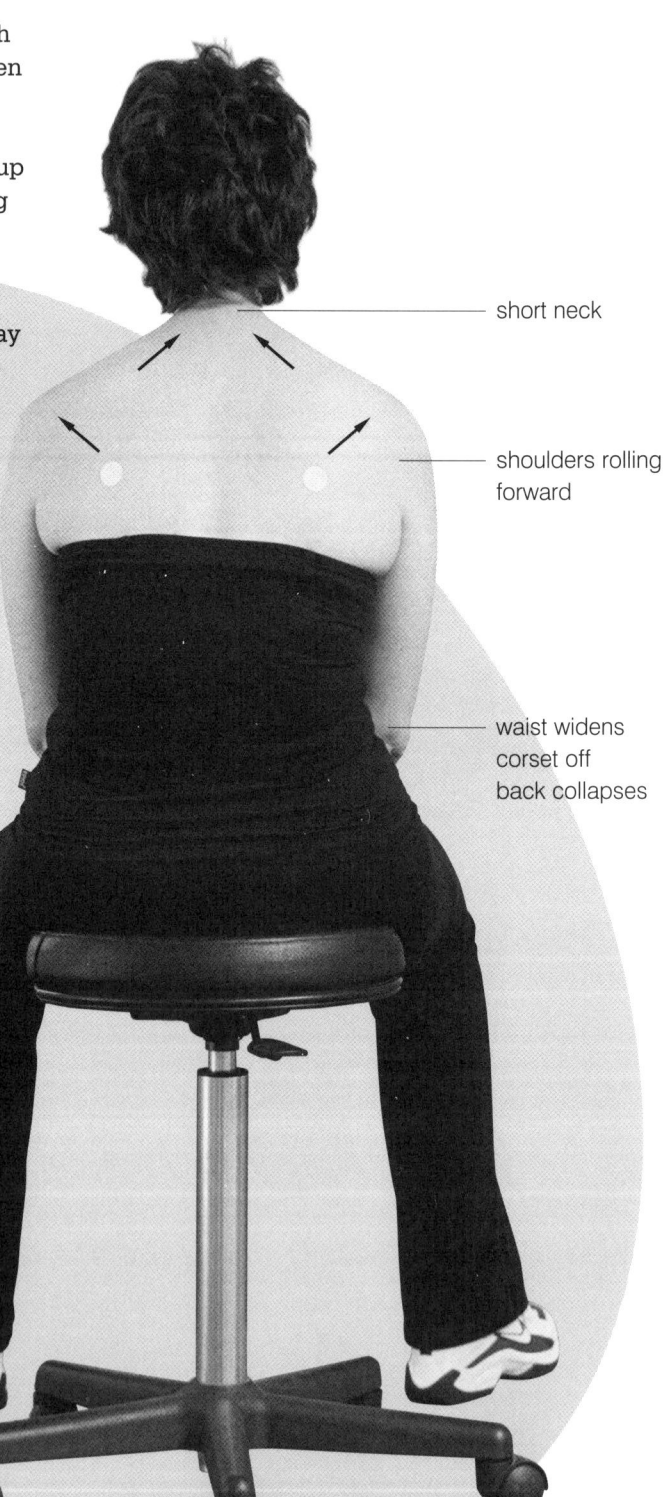

short neck

shoulders rolling forward

waist widens corset off back collapses

back

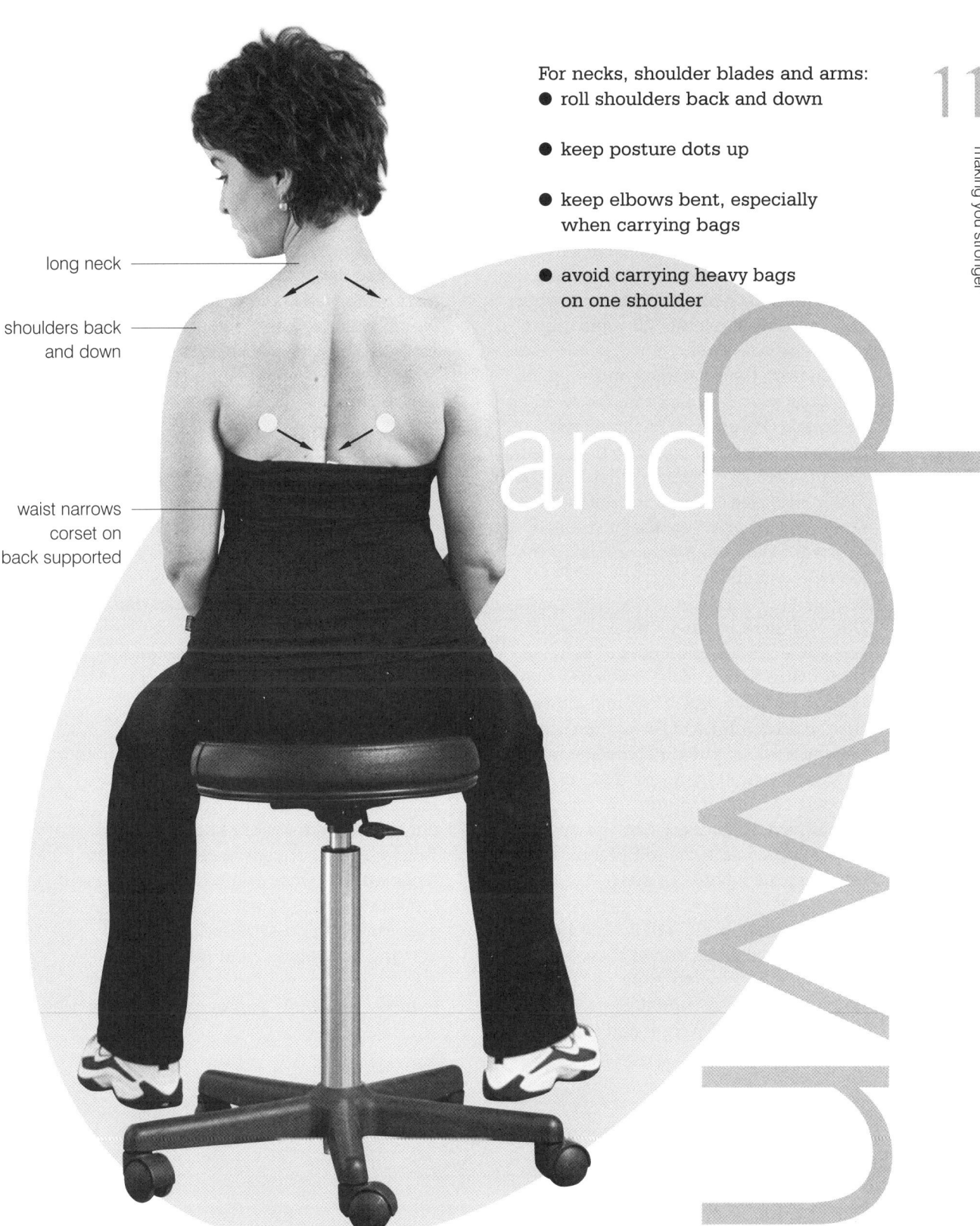

For necks, shoulder blades and arms:
● roll shoulders back and down

● keep posture dots up

● keep elbows bent, especially
when carrying bags

● avoid carrying heavy bags
on one shoulder

long neck

shoulders back
and down

waist narrows
corset on
back supported

115

making you stronger

and

up

and

down

Conclusion

For many people with chronic back pain, there comes a time when they start to think that the discomfort will be around for good. This can be especially worrying for younger people who think that if they feel this bad in their 20s and 30s, then what will it be like in another 20 years time?

Fortunately, the strategies and skills in this book provide a program for avoiding back pain. Fixing your back will not happen instantly. It will take time, thought and practice for structures that have been long underused to learn to switch on again and for muscles that have been overworked for years to stop taking the load off your spine.

Don't be disheartened if intermittently you still endure acute bouts of pain. Underlying your muscle imbalance may be injured ligaments, discs and joints that could continue to be a little sore every once in a while. The difference is, now you will have a strategy to call upon to help support painful structures. For example, if your back is aching when you sit, then use your pain as a cue to BBB and lift your dots and see what happens.

Gradually your brain will learn what eases your pain and what brings it on. Your back will become a very different back. It will be balanced, supported and stronger, so it will recover more quickly and be able to take more load before it gets sore again.

Gaining confidence in your back will improve many other aspects of your life. When you are in pain you don't feel like moving much, much less exercising. Once you feel better, you can think about increasing your general fitness levels, which will also benefit your back. The more sedentary your life, the more critical it is for you to keep moving to keep your back strong.

Always use the strategies you have learned: lift your dots, keep your hibiscus steady and turn your corset on. Soon you will feel better about yourself than you've felt in years. Many of my clients often comment that people ask if they've lost weight when they have been in the program for some time. The combined effects of better posture, more toned muscles and a feeling of wanting to do more can give you a whole new lease on life.

Remember that every back can be fixed to some extent and you don't have to put up with the misery of chronic pain. Taking control of your back pain is very empowering. Once you have incorporated the strategies in this book into your everyday life and acquired new ways of using your spine, your deep muscle corsets and your limbs, you will be able to enjoy your body and get moving again.

Enjoy a balanced, supported, stronger back.

Acknowledgments

This book is the culmination of the work and input of many, many people.
I would like to express my gratitude to the following individuals in particular.

To my commissioning and project editor Jill Brown, whose commitment, honesty
and vision is the strength behind the project. To Ingo Voss whose design work is
so beautiful and whose good-natured patience is always valued. To Jon Reid for
the creativity and life in the photography.

To Hans Roos, Zelda Hammen, Manny Edmonds, Requel Trevillion and
Bryony Hobson for their smiling faces and wonderful energy in the photographs.

To Dr Seamus Dalton, Rehabilitation Physician, for his analytical and perceptive
insights into back pain and movement. His input and support hasvebeen invaluable
in the creation and teaching of the framework.

To Gillian Marcham, my colleague who taught me so much about the pelvic floor.
To Sally Nield, Physiotherapist, who has let me sound out ideas with her for many
years and has given me such honest and balanced feedback.

To my staff, Melissa Partington, Melinda Luck, Shelagh Baker, Mairi Langton,
Requel Trevillion, Jo Wild and Zelda Hammen who have helped to workshop
and teach all the concepts, analysed and observed patients and have been
so willing to help the program grow and evolve.

To my assistant Justine Cooper for her positive outlook and support.

References

Allison, G, Kendall et al. The Role of the Diaphragm during Abdominal Hollowing Exercises. **Australian Journal of Physiotherapy,1998, vol 44, no 2, p 95-102**

Bendix AF, Bendix T. Can it be Predicted which Patients with Chronic Low Back Pain should be offered Tertiary Rehabilitation in a Functional Restoration Program? A Search for Demographic, Socioeconomic and Physical Predictors. Spine,1998, vol 23, p 1775-83, discussion p 1783-4

Bigos SJ, Battie MC, Spengler DM. A Prospective Study of Work Perception and Psychosocial Factors Affecting the Report of Back Injury. Spine, 1991, vol 16, p 1-6

Deyo RA, Rainville J, Kent DL. What can the History and Physical Examination tell us about Low Back Pain? JAMA, 1992, vol 286, p 760-765

Faas A. Exercises: Which Ones are Worth Trying, for Which Patients and When? Spine, 1996, vol 21, p 2787-2879

Frost H et al. A Fitness Program for Patients with Chronic Low Back Pain. 2 year Follow up of a Randomised Controlled Trial. Pain, 1998, vol 75, p 273-279

Hides JA, Richardson CA, Jull GA. Multifidus Muscle Recovery is not Automatic after Resolution of Acute First Episode Low Back Pain. Spine, 1996, vol 21, (23), p 2763-2769

Hides JA et al. Multifidus Muscle Rehabilitation Decreases Recurrence of Symptoms Following First Episode Low Back Pain. Proceeding 1996 National Physiotherapy Congress. July 17-19 1996, p 43-45

Hides JA et al. Evidence of Lumbar Multifidus Muscle Wasting Ipsilateral to Symptoms in Patients with Acute/Subacute Low Back Pain. Spine, 1994, vol 19, no 2, p 165-172

Hodges PW. The Brain, Pain, Muscles and Joint Stability: Fitting the Puzzle together. Congress Proceedings Fifth Annual International APA Congress,1998, p 108-111

Hodges PW, Richardson CA. Inefficient Muscular Stabilisation of the Lumbar Spine associated with Low Back Pain: A Motor Control Evaluation of Transversus Abdominis. Spine, 1996, vol 21, p 2640-2650

Hodges PW. Current Opinion of the Function of Transversus Abdominis. An annotated Bibliography of Papers Investigating Transversus Abdominus. Australian Physiotherapy Association, Manual Therapy Special Group Newsletter, Nov 1998, vol 3, p 8-11

Hodges PW, Richardson CA. Contraction of the Abdominal Muscles associated with Movement of the Lower Limb. Physical Therapy, 1997, 77, p 132-144

Indahl A, Velund L, Reikeraas O. Good Prognosis for Low Back Pain when left Untampered. Spine, 1995, vol 20, p 473-477

Koes BW, Bouter LM, Beckerman H, van der Heijden GJMG, Knipschild PG. Physiotherapy Exercises and Back Pain - a Blinded Review. British Medical Journal, 1991, vol 302, p 1572-1576

Lord S, Castell S. Effect of Exercise on Balance, Strength and Reaction Time in Older People. Australian Journal of Physiotherapy, 1994, vol 40, no 2, p 83-88

Luoto S, Heliovaara M, Alaranta H. Static Back Endurance and the Risk of low-back pain. Clinical Biomechanics, 1995, vol 10, p 323-324

Maher C, Latimer J, Refshauge K. Prescription of Activity for Low Back Pain. What works? Australian Journal of Physiotherapy, 1999, vol 45, p 1121-132

Mulder T. Current Motor Control Theories: Implications for Rehabilitation. Congress Proceedings Fifth International APA Congress, 1998, p 92-94

Noe DA, Mostardi RA, Jackson ME, Portersfield JA, Askew MJ. Myoelectric Activity and Sequencing of Selected Trunk Muscles during Isokinetic Lifting. Spine, 1992, vol 17 (2), p 225

O'Sullivan PB, Twomey L, Allison G. Dysfunction of the Neuro-Muscular System in the Presence of Back Pain — Implications for Physical Therapy Management. Journal of Manual and Manipulative Therapy, 1997, vol 5, no 1, p 20-26

O'Sullivan PB, Twomey L, et al. Altered Patterns of Abdominal Muscle Activation in Patients with Chronic Low Back Pain. Australian Journal of Physiotherapy, 1997, vol 43, no 2, p 42

Proceedings 7th Scientific Conference. International Federation of Orthopaedic Manipulative Therapists (IFOMT). Perth, Western Australia. 2000 KP Singer (ed) The Centre for Musculoskeletal Studies, The University of Western Australia

Quint U, Wilkie HJ. Importance of the Intersegmental Trunk Muscles for the Stability of the Lumbar Spine. A Biomechanical Study. Spine, 1998, vol 23 (18), p 1937-45

Richardson CA et al. Muscle Control — Pain Control. What Exercises would you Prescribe? Manual Therapy, 1995, p 2-10, Pearson Professional

Sahrmann SA. Diagnosis and Treatment of Movement – Related Pain Syndromes Associated with Muscle and Movement Imbalances. 1997, Course Manual

Shacklock MO, Central Pain Mechanisms. A New Horizon in Manual Therapy. Australian Journal of Physiotherapy, 1999, vol 45, p 83-92

Congress Proceedings 6th International Physiotherapy Congress May 2000. Canberra ACT Australia, Australian Physiotherapy Association

Vleeming A et al. A New Light on Low Back Pain. The Self Locking Mechanism of the Sacroiliac Joints and its Implications for Sitting, Standing and Walking. Congress Proceedings Fifth International APA Congress, 1998, p 57-76